Ready to Go → Service Projects

140 Ways for Youth Groups to Lend a Hand

**Ann Saylor &
Susan Ragsdale**

08 09 10 11 12 13 14 15 16 17– 10 9 8 7 6 5 4 3 2 1

MANUFACTURED IN THE UNITED STATES OF AMERICA

Managing Editor: Crys Zinkiewicz
Design Manager: Keely Moore
Editor: Josh Tinley
Production Editor: Susan Heinemann

Designer: Keely Moore
Cover Design: Keely Moore

Acknowledgements

To my mom, Betty Walker Ragsdale (December 26, 1931–September 7, 2007), who exemplified what it means to serve others with whatever gifts one has, both with words and action . . . and food! By her presence, her welcoming hugs, her genuine smile, her open hospitality, and simple acts of kindness she offered love freely to all who came within her world. She was amazing. I pray that I can serve others by love and action as graciously as she did.

—Susan

This book is dedicated to the Armistead, Chapman, Murray, Saylor, Sheppard, Truss, and Young families, who model amazing hospitality, service, and love; to my mom and dad (Tom and Carol Bailey), who challenged me to serve and lead wholeheartedly, with confidence and determination; to my husband, Dan Saylor, who always encourages me to pursue my wildest dreams; and to my three children, Daniel, Brendan, and Anna Kate—may you learn at a young age to share Christ's love with others through service.

—Ann

Many voices contributed to this book's message. In particular we would like to thank Keith Coss, Jacquie Watlington, Anderson Williams, Sharon Williams (no relation to Anderson), David Kelly-Hedrick, Mikkee Hall, Tony Ganger, Berry Brooks, Julie Stevens, Amanda Smith, Ann Hilary Hanly, and Karen Ragsdale for their insights, knowledge, first-hand experiences, memories, and wisdom. This book is incredibly richer for having your voices reflected throughout its pages! Diane Blum and Mike Waldrop, our walking Bible concordances and story keepers, thank you for keeping us as biblically straight as possible and helping find just the right passages. Our prayer is that Christ, the ultimate servant who has transformed us, will use this book to gather others to himself and to ignite Kingdom living more fully here on earth as it is in heaven.

To the team at Abingdon Youth: Crys Zinkiewicz, Josh Tinley, Susan Heinemann, and Keely Moore, thanks for the support and for making our work better. Finally, if it weren't for Ellen Zinkiewicz saying, "You've got to meet my mom," none of this would have happened.

—Susan and Ann

About the Writers

Susan Ragsdale and **Ann Saylor** are nationally recognized trainers, conference presenters and program consultants in the youth and community development field, as well as being authors. As co-founders of the Center for Asset Development at the YMCA of Middle Tennessee, they have coached and trained numerous youth-serving agencies and schools on developing and empowering youth and youth leaders, team building, and service-learning. Their first book, *Great Group Games: 175 Boredom-Busting, Zero-Prep Team Builders for All Ages,* went into its second printing within five months of its release date.

Susan Ragsdale has more than 16 years of experience in the youth and community development field with the YMCA of Middle Tennessee, where she's been involved with a variety of teen leadership and inner-city outreach programs both locally and nationally with the YMCA of USA. Susan lives in Nashville, Tennessee, with her husband, Pete, and their two dogs.

Ann Saylor has developed and directed service-learning programs for multiple organizations since 1994, including Points of Light Foundation, Tennessee 4-H, Volunteer Tennessee, and Harpeth Hall School. She has published more than 150 articles about youth leadership, service-learning, developmental assets, and personal balance. Ann and her husband, Dan, have three children (Daniel, Brendan, and Anna Kate) in live in Pleasant View, Tennessee.

Contents

Easy-to-use sessions that you can use for exploring the value of service, what Scripture has to say, what gifts each person in your group brings to service, as well as for understanding your group and beginning to explore the community

Topical issues including sample service project ideas, reflection questions, prayers, Scriptures, stories about youth in service, and resources for further study

Introduction

The term *service* is everywhere. We service our cars; we expect good service at restaurants; corporations teach good customer service; young people join the military service; we attend services on Sundays, ask for room service, and fill up at service stations. The term is a part of our vernacular and culture.

When *service* is used in the context of helping others, various images may come to mind: places of need (such as rainforests, the Darfur region of the Sudan, or famine-stricken regions); people we hold in high regard for their service (such as Gandhi, Martin Luther King, Jr., or Mother Teresa); local community organizations (such as the food bank, rescue mission, or Habitat for Humanity); or people picking up trash wearing orange vests.

What comes to mind has everything to do with our experiences, exposure, and frame of reference. If one has not been actively involved in service or worked with others, then he or she may perceive service as a punishment or as something that requires extraordinary skill or calling, not as something we all can do every day in large and small ways.

But what is true service?

True service is a a response to a call from deep within us. Our excuses not to serve are often defined by external, cultural factors. By contrast, those who serve are willing to do so, with or without the support of the cultural structures.

All of us have gifts and skills that count. All people can make a difference with the gifts they have. We do not have to be Mother Teresa or Dr. Martin Luther King, Jr.; and we do not need to use them as an excuse for not getting involved. ("I'm not like them. I don't have the same character or skills.") Instead, their actions should inspire us. We should be ourselves, using our talents, gifts, knowledge, and resources for the common good wherever we can. In big or small ways, it adds up. The task is simply to be present and to love and serve with compassion.

SERVICE AND FAITH: BECOMING SERVANT LEADERS

Service is a core expression of the church, passed on to its members, young and old. The church upholds this way of life through acts of compassion, mercy, love, and justice that help individuals as well as address social and community ills. We can be thankful that the church is one of the cultural institutions that promotes and fuels service and that many faith traditions agree that service is part of being fully human.

Within the church many youth groups perform service projects, knowing instinctively that service is just a good thing to do. Not only will it keep them active, a youth pastor may think, but maybe in the process, some compassion for others will rub off and serving others will become a way of life.

This book seeks to heighten that instinctive knowing with tools, vision, and ideas to create an intentional approach to service that will further develop youth into servant leaders. It begins with knowledge about service-learning.

> Do all the good you can,
> By all the means you can,
> In all the ways you can,
> In all the places you can,
> At all the times you can,
> To all the people you can,
> As long as ever you can.
>
> —John Wesley

Through service-learning, youth will realize their capacities for skills, compassion, and understanding and be commissioned as servant leaders to change the world around them. Maximizing the potential of service-learning takes attentive planning, intentionally involving youth throughout every step of the process, establishing meaning and purpose on the front end and deliberately building in opportunities for reflection throughout.

Use this guide as a tool to stimulate, challenge, and encourage service-learning within your group of young people. Here you'll find practices, stories, and tips that were gathered from pastors, agencies, and others in the youth ministry, both church and secular from around the United States.

Service-learning at its best will equip youth to be servant leaders who grow in faith and address injustices and needs that they see around them today and for the rest of their lives.

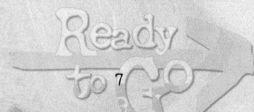

READY-TO-GO SERVICE PROJECTS

Part 1:
The Basics

The following unit is a brief overview of the nuts and bolts of service-learning: what it is, why groups should do it, and how it can help you develop your youth group.

What Is Service-learning?

The term *service-learning* was coined in the 1960s. This core strategy for positive youth development has roots in academic settings. Since the 1960s, it has become fundamental in service and outreach (including programs such as the Peace Corps, VISTA, Points of Light Foundation, National Youth Leadership Council and Youth Service America). This honored practice has helped develop servant leaders now for over forty years.

DEFINITION

Service-learning is a process of learning and doing, doing and learning that engages people in meaningful service while they actively learn from the service experience.

Simply put, service-learning is a 50/50 split: a 50 percent emphasis on taking action and a 50 percent emphasis on learning.

What Service-learning Is:

→ an act of love, hospitality, and justice

→ an act of giving and receiving

→ doing the work to understand the work

→ a way to uncover the root causes of issues and systemic injustices

→ an act of empowerment and liberation

→ a spotlight on the human condition and the connectedness of all persons and all persons' struggles

→ a place for youth to acknowledge their own struggles and see them in a broader social context

→ a mighty equalizer reminding us that we all have something to offer

What Service-learning Is NOT:

→ something to do during our spare time

→ just for the privileged

→ all about feeling good and having fun

→ a one-sided gift

→ an experience to be crammed into a one-hour session

→ a project for adults to plan for young people

See page 42 for a multisensory way to teach service-learning.

When service-learning is done properly, you can expect higher quality in the projects you undertake. Youth will grow when they are involved in a project from the start and when we acknowledge the gifts that they have to make change happen. And when a youth group involves the community, you can expect the experience to be more meaningful both for your group and for the community.

Jacquie Watlington, a school-based service-learning director and former youth pastor, says, "Service can be so powerful. I've seen students who have questioned the existence of God, open up to the possibility of exploring Christianity. I've seen service projects help outsiders find a place where they feel accepted in the youth group. I've seen students respond with a tearful confession and healing from intense anger over parental divorce and abandonment."

Why Emphasize Learning?

We learn every day—from our friends, what we read, what we watch on television, what we see on the Internet, and from nature. But there is a difference between subconscious learning—simply absorbing things in without running them through any filters or checkpoints—and intentional learning—deliberately drawing out lessons and learning to examine, clarify and hold, or dismiss one's experiences. Service-learning intentionally uses service experiences to teach about life, society, values, and self.

This learning involves deliberately setting aside time for discussing newly gained insights and determining talents. If there is no time to honor learning or capture "a-ha" moments—if there is no reflection—then it is not service-learning; it is simply service. Learning and reflection transform service into service-learning, and participants into servant leaders.

Why Do Service-learning?

When talking about servant leadership, we can take our cue from **Matthew 25:31-40** ("Whatever you did for one of the least of these . . . , you did for me" [NIV]). It answers the question, Who are the people of God? The people of God are those who live out the command to "love your neighbor as yourself" (**Leviticus 19:18**) in their daily lives.

"They didn't know they were doing it for Jesus," said Mike, a pastor in Tennessee, when referring to the youth he works with. "In fact, [the righteous people in **Matthew 25**] were surprised when Jesus said this is what [they had done]. The ones who didn't do the things Jesus described . . . were also surprised. Their reaction was, 'Gee, if we had known it was you, we would have done it.' Here Jesus gives us a model for what it means to be faithful, to be servant leaders."

Youth become better servant leaders when they know that by serving others, they are serving Jesus and making God's kingdom real on earth.

Compassion and Understanding

Reflection and capturing "a-ha" moments can help youth understand and have compassion for those they are serving.

My friend Keith helped articulate how compassion can enhance servant leadership. When discussing servant leadership with Keith, we explored embracing people with challenges—physical, material, and otherwise—and the importance of understanding their challenges from their perspective, to walk through their world with them, to indeed develop a sense of compassion, which literally means to "suffer with" in Latin. (For those of you who would like to study this area further, try Henri Nouwen's book *Compassion*).

Keith told me a story about his father-in-law, Sam, in his last year of life fighting emphysema. Though confined to a wheelchair, Sam was still imparting valuable lessons of wisdom, compassion, and understanding about life and its challenges. Keith recalled:

> I was out shopping with my in-laws. My mother-in-law was piling stuff into Sam's lap, loading him up with packages. This was a fairly normal routine for the two of them. A woman came by and noticed my father-in-law all loaded up.
>
> When the lady saw Sam sitting there all weighed down with stuff, she said, "Oh, I'm so sorry they've piled you up with all that stuff."
>
> He smiled at her and said, "It's OK" and left it at that. The woman left.
>
> He told me afterwards that she simply didn't understand. Holding the packages in his lap and helping his wife shop was one of the ways he still felt useful.

Keith went on to tell me the lessons he gleaned from Sam about living with disabilities:

> It's not about holding a door open for a person in a wheelchair. It's something else. It's, "Come into my world as much as I go into your world."

Know me. Be in a relationship with me. Understand me. Allow me the opportunity to know you, be in a relationship with you, and understand you.

Keith explained that we need to enter the world of the people we serve:

> Once we go into their world, we become comfortable. I became comfortable with Sam's world and have become comfortable with other people's worlds as well. Part of my life now includes having friends who choose to be homeless. I have become comfortable being around guys who smell, who dress funny, who live in cardboard houses. I have become comfortable around guys who have mix-and-match clothes or no shoes. I have entered their world, and they have allowed me to discover it and make it a part of mine.

Jesus said in **James 1:27,** "Religion that is pure and undefiled before God, the Father, is this: to care for orphans and widows in their distress, and to keep oneself unstained by the world." This is what he meant: We are to visit them in *their* distress. His instructions were for us to go out and know our neighbors where they are, as they are, and simply to love them. Much of servant leadership is about presence, being with others, and sharing their lives.

We take the gift of ourselves and share that gift with others, in love.

Presence, love, hospitality, compassion—these are what serving others is all about. And the reward for the labor bears fruit of the same.

Getting Up Close and Personal: The Relationship Factor

Service-learning addresses the problems that have come with technology. The current problems of obesity, depression, and isolation in America are linked in part to the amount of time people spend on the computer, playing video games, or on the couch in front of the television. With more time spent in the virtual world and less in the real world, many individuals suffer not only from lack physical activity but also isolation from the community and natural world around us. Technology, while useful in many ways, can be addictive and confining.

"Technology makes it tough because [youth] spend time doing with their hands and not spending time with others," said Diane, a senior pastor in Nashville, Tennessee. "With technology you're not engaging the fives senses, nor the sixth sense of intuition for that matter ... you get an impoverished version of use of tactile, visual, and audible. "

Service-learning helps youth get up close and personal. It gives youth a chance to know and experience with all of their senses (not just the visual and audible senses stimulated by virtual reality) the environment around them as well as its people, plants, and animals. It offers a much needed opportunity for youth to get up, get out, touch, feel, explore, know, and grapple with the tangible world right outside their doors.

Along with engaging youth through a variety of stimuli, service-learning's emphasis on both doing and learning allows young people (who are used to going from one thing to another by the click of a mouse) to truly get to know their world.

In addition to helping youth see the world for what it truly is, service-learning can help youth develop skills in interacting with others. Dianne, an M.Ed. and twenty-plus-year tutor and consultant for North Carolina school systems, has noticed the affect that technology has on relational skills in youth. From the I.Q. tests she has helped give, she observes "that the relational skills (their understanding of cause and effect, outcomes) are going

14

down and their performance skills (the ability to manipulate visual information) are going up."

Service-learning is a primary experience, a first-hand encounter that involves direct interaction with the people and world around us. It fully engages all the wisdom, senses, and faculties of those involved. This live encounter provides opportunities for relationships to build and understanding to take place. Service-learning can get participants out of their chairs (or off their phones, beds, or couches) and into their senses, fully engaging them in hands-on experiences that enrich and close the gap of isolation and inactivity.

Thus, service-learning can help young people realize and recognize their connection to a wider community, a community of life that is vivid, real, and dynamic, a connection that will never short-circuit or crash irreparably.

Bringing Out the Assets in Your Youth

Service-learning is, by its very nature, one of the best way to build Developmental Assets™ in youth. Developmental Assets™ are relationships, experiences, attitudes, skills, and competencies that help them become caring, competent, healthy individuals. (See the chart on the next page.)

They include:

→ support
→ empowerment
→ boundaries and expectations
→ constructive use of time
→ commitment to learning
→ positive values
→ social competencies
→ positive identity

For more on Developmental Assets™ go to *www.search-institute.org.* This website includes tips, ideas, and resources for helping youth thrive.

These assets are based on research conducted by Search Institute, a leader in the nation for positive youth development practices, located in Minneapolis, Minnesota.

Search Institute's research plays out: The more assets young people have, the more likely they are to thrive (to volunteer, be leaders, and appreciate diversity) and the less likely they are to engage in behaviors or activities that could be harmful to themselves or others (to join a gang, take drugs, or drink). The bottom line is: The more assets, the better! And service-learning is one of the best ways to build those vital building blocks that youth need in their lives.

"Service leads to positive identity, empowerment, and other assets that are critical to healthy youth development," says Sharon Williams, a career youth worker who serves as YMCA consultant with youth workers across the United States. "Young people who engage in true service-learning are better off than young people who don't."

"Meaningful service truly comes from the heart. Nurture that ethic from an early age."

—Sharon Williams

This chart shows how Search Institute's Developmental Assets™ and service-learning work hand in hand:

Asset	Definition	Service-learning Connection
Support	Young people feel welcomed, loved, cared for, appreciated, and accepted by the people who surround them.	Working side by side on projects together can help cement caring relationships.
Empowerment	Young people feel valued and valuable. They have opportunities to contribute in meaningful ways and do so when they feel safe.	As youth tap into their personal power for making a difference, they become resources and are able to recognize their capabilities.
Boundaries and Expectations	Young people have a sense of what is expected of them and are encouraged to give their best. They know what is OK to do and what isn't; they know the rules and the consequences.	When the group develops ground rules, it ensures that everyone takes responsibility for his or her own actions and clear expectations can challenge them to new growth.
Constructive Use of Time	Young people have enriching opportunities to pursue interests and passions and to develop skills with other people, young and old alike, both through programs outside their school and by time at home.	In crafting their own projects, youth get to use their time in ways of their choosing, thus engaging their interests, passions, hearts, and minds in what they want to pursue.
Commitment to Learning	Young people develop a lifelong commitment to learning.	Building links between education and service projects can serve to strengthen young people's desire to learn and to apply what they are learning to issues they care about.
Positive Values	Young people develop core values and principles that guide their choices and that shape their interactions with others.	Through service-learning, youth are able to explore, name, and claim the values they hold while examining how theirs compare to the world in which they live.
Social Competencies	Young people develop life skills to build caring relationships and to make positive, healthy decisions.	Through service-learning, youth have opportunities to practice and develop valuable skills while serving others.
Positive Identity	Young people develop a strong sense of their own power, purpose, and worth and see hope for the future. Working side by side on projects together can help cement caring relationships.	Through service to others, youth are able to realize their power to make things happen and to realize their value and worth. In essence, they can discover their God-given talents and their place in this world.

Group-Involvement Checklist

To ensure that you are using asset-based service-learning (instead of just getting the job done), look at how you manage your time with your youth group:

→ Do you make sure that everyone is included?

→ Do you make sure that all participants feel safe?

→ Do you ensure that each person has a meaningful role to contribute?

→ Do you discuss values and help youth gain social skills they need for life (friendship skills, conflict-resolution skills, and so on)?

→ Do you affirm their gifts and their value as human beings and as children of God?

→ Do you give them opportunities to contribute and develop their own sense of personal power?

→ Do you help youth make connections between service and faith?

If you can answer yes to all or most of these questions, you are well on your way to helping the young people in your group become their very best.

What Is the Service-learning Process?

Service-learning has four stages:

→ **GETTING STARTED:** knowing what you want to do, setting goals, and mapping a plan to get there with everyone on board

→ **TAKING ACTION:** getting things done, moving from thinking to doing

→ **REFLECTING:** replaying those memorable scenes, capturing the oohs, ahhs, a-ha's, and "Oh, yeah!" moments

→ **CELEBRATING:** ending with a splash, such as a ceremony, group hug, or campfire song

GETTING STARTED

Before taking any action, think about these four things:

1. Your group: Who are they? What are they interested in? What are their passions, skills, and interests?

2. Your community: Who are they? What do they need? How can they be involved as actors for community change?

3. Set the stage for learning: What do the youth want to learn or gain from this experience? What do you as the youth leader want them to gain or understand? What does the community want us to know or do?

4. Know and identify your resources, needs, and a plan: What are they? What will do? Who is responsible for each step? By when?

Getting Started is all about becoming more familiar with your group and your community. What do you want to know and what do you need to know before you dive into service? Use this planning stage to let youth lead and define this process. If this phase is all adult driven, you will lose some of your energy and maybe some of your youth. This initial step of questioning sets the stage for young people to have true ownership of service-learning.

Your Group

You want to have a sense of your students and what they are all about. What makes them tick? How do they love to spend their free time? What talents and skills do they possess? What areas of interest do they show? What passions do they have? Where could they see themselves making a difference and enjoying it or feeling a sense of accomplishment and pride? What area of the community would they like to learn more about (because they are interested in it, it's an issue that is important in their lives, they are thinking about a career in that area, or simply "just because")?

As you explore your youth group's interests, passions, and talents, you accomplish three things:

1. You get their attention. When you sincerely ask youth what they think, what they want to do, and what they want to change and when you act on that input, they'll realize that your group is different from groups where they're expected to passively follow the leader.

2. You help them think about and recognize their own gifts. Not everyone can easily name her or his own skills and talents; you may have to help by pointing out gifts you see (with group input to further encourage and build up each youth). Nor do many people recognize how their knowledge and experiences make them experts in certain areas. (For example, teens are experts in being a teenager. A teenager who lives in a low-income neighborhood knows more about what that neighborhood needs than anyone else because he or she lives there; the teen knows about the community store, church, and neighbors with all the treasures and trials germane to the area.)

3. You shape a service experience with them that incorporates their interests, expertise, experiences, and passions, further solidifying their buy-in, participation, and ownership.

Taking the time to pull in the group and start with them as resources and actors in what will take place kicks off the service-learning in the right way.

This involvement from the beginning is one of the distinctions between service and service-learning. With service by itself, the temptation (and the norm) is to load a van full of youth bodies, take them to a site, dump them off, and let them go to work as volunteer zombies. Service-learning, by contrast, engages youth from the get-go in identifying needs, setting goals, planning, and shaping the service experiences. Regardless of prior experience, knowledge, or background, all students contribute and are empowered to make a difference.

Your Community

Knowing the community you want to work with as well as you know your group is crucial.

→ Step 1: Define the scope of your community.

Determine the community area you are serving. Is the community a small geographic area, or an entire state? Is it an agency across the street, or a sister church around the world? Is it the street your church is on? your neighborhood block? a nursing home where members of your church live? How you define your community is up to you and the group. Your community can be as narrow as the empty lot next door or as broad as the world. You decide, keeping in mind your group's interests, resources, means, and desires. Remember that anything is possible and that desire and passion can go a long way to overcome financial shortcomings.

→ Step 2: Get to know your community.

Once you determine your geographical community area, your youth group

A fourth-grade class in Aurora, Colorado, made a difference in the fight against modern-day slavery. After learning about the history of slavery in the United States, the teacher told the students about slavery in Sudan. The children were appalled the institution was still active and asked what they could do about it. They contacted an agency and watched a news story about the plight of women and children in Sudan who were sold as slaves. Determining to battle this horrible injustice, the children collected money from family, neighbors, and the community. After a *CBS Evening News* broadcast on slavery in the Sudan that highlighted the class, more contributions poured in. The children raised over $50,000 for the agency to purchase over 1,000 slaves and set them free.

This story reminds us that we can accomplish anything we want if we set our course to action and stay steadfast to our vision.

should link arms with the people who live and work there. Don't cultivate or encourage a Lone Ranger attitude—that of riding in on a horse to "save" the community. You are not there to simply give charity; that attitude is not helpful in the long run. Instead, engage community members in problem solving and work together to create solutions, seeking to create a healthier and stronger community for everyone.

"We have to see ourselves as connected and dependent on each other," said Mike, a pastor in Tennessee. "Service-learning breaks the barriers between 'us' and 'them,' to it just being 'us' together. It spotlights the human condition where we can identify with each other."

David, a youth director in Seattle, Washington, agrees on the importance of learning from those whom one serves and regarding them as equals. "Few of us like to receive help, and most of us have a really difficult time asking for help; yet over the course of our lives, it is highly probable that we will all be receivers as well as givers," David said. "How can we act on both sides of this equation with grace and dignity?" Remembering our own natural resistance to receiving help reminds us of the importance of engaging everyone as equal givers and contributors.

So have your group spend time asking questions and having conversations with the members of the community area where they want to help:

• Who's in the community?

• What businesses, agencies, and individual leaders (moms, pastors, young people, bus drivers, store clerks, and so on) can help?

• What is their experience in the community?

• What issues do they think need to be addressed?

• What hinders the community from being healthy and thriving? What needs aren't being met?

• What are their hopes and dreams for where they live?

• What roles can they play in addressing issues and concerns?

• In what ways do they think your group could work with them to meet needs?

Asking questions and listening can set the stage for social change. This step requires a bit of detective work on your group's part to ensure that the project you ultimately design is one that will meet relevant needs.

→ Step 3: Analyze how your group can meet the community's needs.

Once you've talked with community members and gotten their opinions on pertinent issues, you are ready to start planning your service project.

What needs is your group particularly interested in? Where do your group's hopes and dreams intersect with the hopes and dreams of the people in the community? If no ideas come up immediately, have no fear. Ideas will bubble forth from all the detective work that your group does. As ideas arise, examine each one and determine what your group should do.

As your group narrows down the issues it wants to explore, invite community members to meet with your group to give their perspective on the issues that the community faces; invite them to help out with the project. Then you will know what needs are truly relevant. The involvement of those for whom the issue is crucial increases understanding and compassion.

→ Step 4: Engage the community leaders.

Throughout the process of dreaming and planning, continue to engage people in the community who are working on the issue you've decided to tackle. The expression, "Many hands make light work" is true. How can your group build bridges to people and groups within the community to increase effectiveness? What can your group do to help or partner with people

Imagine that a group of young people in a van passing by an apartment complex every day on their way to their after-school program. "Hey! I know what we can do for our service project," one girl exclaims. "Have you ever noticed that the apartment complex doesn't have a playground? Where do all the kids get to play?" The young people start discussing the idea, getting passionate about providing a safe place for children to play and have fun. The group leader suggests that one of the youth write down the name of the apartment complex and call them to find out whether they are interested in having a playground built for their community.

The next week, that student is bombarded with questions from the eager group. He sheepishly lets them know that the apartment complex is a residence for the elderly and that a playground is not something they need.

This story shows the importance of knowing the community and working side by side with them. In this example, the group has discovered that they have a passion for creating safe play opportunities for young people. The next step is to look around the community to see how that passion can be put to good use to meet real community needs. Can the group lead recreational activities for an after-school group? Can they paint and mulch at an existing playground? Can they plan a field day for kids at their church? Or is there a place in the community that truly does need a playground built as they had hoped to do?

or groups that are already taking a lead in addressing the issue that you've identified? Your youth group cannot make sustainable community change alone; you need cooperation from other people and groups. And they need you.

Set the Stage for Learning

Once you know your group's interests and what community needs you wish to address, set two or three learning goals: One for yourself, one for the group, and one from the community you will be working with in service.

(Picture a three-legged school. Action represents the seat and is propped up by three base legs of support: self, the group, and the community. It takes all three elements working together to support the seat of action and to provide a solid base for growth to take place. If action is missing any one leg of influence, it will become wobbly and unstable.)

Setting learning goals will allow you to keep the group focused, give you something to look back at when the project is done, and help you see changes in attitudes and growth in knowledge and skills.

Consider these questions when setting learning goals:

• How do you personally hope to grow from this experience?

• What do you want to learn about the issue or community from participating in this project?

• What skills or knowledge do you hope to gain from this project?

• When the project is finished, what do you hope to have accomplished?

This process gives youth the freedom to articulate what is important to them and to keep track of their progress. Learning objectives invite them to take charge of their learning experience and to invest themselves more wholeheartedly into what happens.

Resources, a Need, and a Plan

Once objectives are established, map out a plan by identifying available resources and determining what needs to be done.

What resources does the group have? (Resources include skills, talents, connections, and material items.) Whom do you and the group know?

READY-TO-GO SERVICE PROJECTS

What can they supply or have donated? What can they make? This planning not only builds self-confidence and self-awareness of group members; it also builds group identity and helps you as the program leader know the strengths of your youth. In addition, mapping out skills and talents helps youth identify other skills that they want to gain or expand.

What will the group do? What project will meet the needs identified? Many young people are full of ideas about how they want to change the world. Crafting this vision taps into the powers, creativity, and divine spark of your group and stirs hopeful action. Use the Readying Your Hands Activity Plans (pages 42–95) to get your dreaming under way.

Here are some keys to success when generating ideas:

• Accept all ideas, crazy, wild, or otherwise.
• Encourage everyone to participate.
• Draw ideas out of youth who are normally quiet or reluctant to contribute. (You may have to ask them directly for their thoughts.)

Then ask, "What action needs to be taken? Who will be responsible for each step of the action plan?"

Make sure that every person has a role in the action plan, and establish a timeline that tells the owner of each task what he or she needs to do and when.

Remember this old story?

Everybody, Somebody, Nobody, and Anybody

Once upon a time, there were four people. Their names were Everybody, Somebody, Nobody, and Anybody.

Whenever there was an important job to be done, Everybody was sure that Somebody would do it. Anybody could have done it, but Nobody did it.

When Nobody did it, Everybody got angry because it was Everybody's job.

Everybody thought that Somebody would do it, but Nobody realized that Nobody would do it.

So consequently Everybody blamed Somebody when Nobody did what Anybody could have done in the first place.

How true! When left to chance, nobody will do what anybody could have done. Somebody will do it only if he or she owns the task.

Make sure that everyone signs up for a role and has something to contribute to the task.

And finally, ask, "Who else can help?" Do not forget the resource of friends! Actively recruit others to help with the project.

When determining your timeline, consider training, technical needs, orientation, and safety. Are certain tools needed? Does your group know how to use these tools? Is an orientation session needed to discuss what behavior is expected and what is off limits at your project site? Check on all these things before starting your service project.

TAKING ACTION

The taking-action stage provides a platform for learning to take place while doing significant, valuable work for the community—if that work meets real needs. Action can take various forms, such as creative efforts, physical work, lobbying, and writing. Discern which projects match your group's talents, skills, availability, and time frames.

The possibilities for action are endless. Several ideas are included in this book. And these ideas are not ends; they are meant to be springboards for further ideas. Any project that you start should continue as long as it meets a real need.

From Crawling to Walking

Many youth groups have huge dreams to change the world. Your job is to help them start with small, doable service projects (that they can finish in a day or less) and work your way up to bigger, more complex projects (multiple-day projects or ongoing projects). Successfully finishing small projects feeds the group identity and entices the youth to want to do even more. Build on each success, and slowly build up to more time-intensive projects that tap into the strengths and interests of your group.

Think of this progression as crawling to walking to running. Crawl projects are easy to do and yield immediate results. Walk projects take a little more effort and coordination and do not yield immediate results. Run projects require training and committed effort to seeing the project through but are well worth the effort; youth are able to hold off the need for immediate gratification in the interest of effecting change for the common good.

Example: Helping Homeless People

Say, for instance, that your group has decided to do service projects that help homeless persons in your community. Here are examples of small, medium, and large projects that rely on students' creative, organizational, and interpersonal gifts:

Small Project (Crawling): Make placemats. Then help serve a meal at a local rescue mission and leave the placements with the mission as a gift.

Medium Project (Walking): Make sleeping bags for homeless persons in your community. Do research on how to make the sleeping bags, collect sewing supplies and material, organize your workspace, recruit volunteers, and make the sleeping bags. Then work with a local mission or ministry to distribute the bags to homeless persons.

Big Project (Running): Arrange to have homeless people from your community spend the night at your church once a month. Offer your guests a hearty meal and a warm place to sleep. If your community already has a ministry that works with churches to provide shelter for the homeless, contact this ministry and see how your congregation or youth group can get involved. If no such ministry exists, work with city leaders, local rescue missions, and other congregations to get it started. Once it's up and running, you'll need to organize the space, recruit volunteers, come up with a menu, and determine sleeping arrangements.

You can see how this sequence of activities lets youth explore one issue, starting with an easy and quick project and then exploring the issue in deeper and in more complex ways. Start small; then continually build up strengths, talents, and confidence. Over time, you'll be able to do more, tackle bigger community issues, and face bigger challenges and long-term projects.

Youth at the Forefront

Success at any of these stages (crawling, walking, or running) requires empowering youth to take on leadership roles. Make sure that the teens help select leaders and that as many teens as possible have leadership responsibilities. With support, guidance, and clear expectations from you, youth should be at the forefront, running the show with you on the side as a cheerleader. Getting to this point takes dedicated effort on your part to let go of power.

Even though some teens will be designated as leaders, everyone involved in the project needs to regard everyone else as equals. Common, manual labor is a good way to level the playing field. Who cares what neighborhood someone lives in when you're working together to dig a well or stuff envelopes? It's important that youth not only work closely with the other group members but also with members of the community. Working side by side for a common purpose does more to unite and bind people together than any formal get-to-know-you effort. It opens up doors to compassion, understanding, and a realization that you are "all in this together."

Be Prepared

The last key for this stage is to live by the Scout motto to "be prepared." You never know what may go awry. For example:

> A youth group planned to build trails leading down to the lake at a camp. Everything was in place for the project when the van rolled up. The students poured out of the van—including Lisa, who was in a wheelchair. Since Lisa was a long-time member of the group, the others had simply not thought about the challenge for her being where there were no trails yet.

> After a quick huddle, the group (with Lisa's input) determined a meaningful role for her in supporting the group's work of building the trails. Though the group quickly came up with a solution, the adult leaders felt frustrated that they had not thought through this difficulty prior to the event. Nonetheless, they were pleased that the group was able to be flexible and that the day was not lost.

> In the reflection session, Lisa revealed that she was very shy and had never worked on such a project before due to her disability. She had the most fun she had ever had as part of the group and was glad that she had come out for the event.

Fortunately things worked out for Lisa. But the group, with Lisa's help, should have planned beforehand various ways to give Lisa a meaningful role.

REFLECTING

The service-learning projects you undertake may introduce participants to new feelings (maybe even uncomfortable ones), experiences, issues, concerns, and questions. If left unaddressed, all this new stuff may leave the participants more confused or frustrated.

"Reflection," said Sharon Williams, "helps young people realize, 'Wow, I made a difference. I can really make a difference. I have skills and talents to share. I'm a valuable member of my community.'"

Unfortunately, this component of service-learning is the one that is most frequently neglected. But reflection is crucial for learning, which is half of service-learning. In fact, describing reflection as the third stage of service-learning is somewhat of a misnomer. Reflection can and should take place before, during, *and* after a project.

Pre-reflection (done before a project takes place) lets you see where your group is going into a project. It lets them verbalize the preconceived ideas that they have about a particular issue or group of people. It establishes a baseline of feelings, attitudes, and understanding that you can revisit after the service experience.

Action-reflection allows you to see how everyone is doing. Are they OK with their assignments? Do changes need to be made as to who does what so that the work load and fun load are shared equally and so that everyone gets to experience variety? Is the group making progress toward meeting the goals that were set? If not, is that OK? Do you need to address any challenges?

Post-reflection involves looking back at all that was done and talking about it. How are the students' feelings, understanding, and attitudes different from how they were pre-project? What new perspective have the youth gained regarding the issue, project, or community? What have they learned? Did your service project accomplish your goals? Did it meet real needs? What do your youth wish they would have done better? What else needs to be done to address the issue at hand?

Note: During the service project, youth may laugh, be scared, or make jokes because they are uncomfortable in this new situation. Reflection can help them deal with their fears in a safe place.

Vary the reflection activities to engage everyone, because everyone learns differently. Ask your youth about how the experience challenged their values and preconceptions. Did the experience reveal any biases or prejudices that the youth were not aware of beforehand? How have they grown in compassion and understanding?

Mike, a pastor in Tennessee, suggested, "Involve everyone in the reflection time—partners, youth, recipients, everyone. What are their hopes and dreams and feelings about what was done? It's really helpful to involve them in reflection as well as action. It continues to break down barriers and build connections."

Again, as with other stages of service learning, let youth lead reflection activities. Remember to keep the space safe (no ideas are bad ones, what is said in the group stays in the group, no laughing at others, and so on).

An Example of the Value of Reflection

The youth group was going to spend the day feeding the homeless. For many in the group this was a first-time experience. The youth came from all economic levels. The group sat down before going over to the mission to serve food to talk about what they thought the experience was going to be like. Their concerns included, "Everyone will be dirty," "they will smell," and "they are dangerous."

The group went and bought the special treats they had planned: hamburgers from a local fast food place. Although the youth had planned to stick together, more homeless persons than anticipated showed up and one of the youth, Cathy, got separated from the others physically and visually. A little more than nervous, she later said that she had felt panicked and was concerned that harm could come her way. She held her peace, however, and simply kept distributing hamburgers to people as they came up. When she got low on burgers, she made the announcement that there were only a few left. To her surprise, she said later, she noted how the crowd checked with each other to see who had not had food yet. They distributed the burgers around, and people began to share.

As we spent time reflecting on the day's event, we looked again at what we thought was going to happen and what had actually happened. Cathy, who was from a well-off family, was the first one to claim the change of her own perspective. She laughed at how she had thought that homeless people were dangerous. She recapped her feelings of panic when she got separated from the group and her amazement at the generosity, respect, and care that she saw exhibited by the homeless during lunch both for one another and for her. She shook her head. "This experience," she said, "shot my preconceived notions. I thought I knew what this was going to be like, but I was wrong."

The group then began to wonder how many other things they had been wrong about. Reflection provided the perfect closing for their project.

CELEBRATING

Last but not least comes the party! This stage is for recognizing and celebrating growth, accomplishments, meeting goals, making new friends, learning new things, developing new skills, conquering fears, and so on.

Recognition affirms diligence, group identity, and teamwork; applauds skills; and honors growth, contributions, and talents. Celebration adds energy and momentum to the project's finish. It reinforces the importance of the roles everyone played in making things happen. This renewal of energy catapults the group into the next phase of action and the next project!

Include the youth in designing celebratory moments. Consider designating a memory-maker (or team) to capture moments on film and to jot down quotations throughout the process to use in a fun way later. Vary the ways you celebrate: pizza party, ceremony, show and tell, article for the paper, presentation at church, you name it!

Jacquie Watlington said, "One of my favorite end-of-a-mission-trip experiences is to have a foot-washing ceremony together, each youth washing and being washed, blessing and being blessed. It is a beautiful act of humility, service, and honor, connecting those who have come to know each other in new ways through serving side by side."

She also suggested, "Use pictures, pictures, pictures (or video). Kids love to see themselves in pictures, and the shots are a great debriefing tool when you return. We always have a 'reunion party' the week after we return. Each student brings copies of [his or her] pictures to share. We reflect, celebrate, and talk about our week of transition back into our 'normal routine.' This is a great point at which to talk about living a missionary life and that being engaged in the transforming work of Jesus is not restricted to dedicated times of service or missions. The departing challenge is always to be attentive to where God is at work around them and to look for ways to be a servant at the grocery, at school, to their teammates, to their family members, and all those they come in contact with."

What You Need to Know: A Quick Reference Cheat Sheet

This guide sums up the pertinent points of the cycle of service-learning:

Real world, real times	What needs do we see around us? What are the pressing concerns that need to be addressed to make life better for others, for the community, for the natural world and its population? What injustices need to be made right?
Vision	What could this community look like if we made it even better?
Tapping our power	What gifts do we have? What talents, resources, skills, and passions do we bring to make things better? What is our knowledge of the issue? What do we have to offer?
Tapping more power	What needs do our neighbors in the community see that need to be met? What gifts, talents, resources, skills, passions, knowledge, and experience do they have that they can offer to make things better?
Getting organized	What do we need to do to get started? Make a list, make a plan, decide who does what, and set goals and dates.
Recruiting others	Who can help?
Action	What are we waiting for? Go ahead and start doing meaningful work!
Reflection	What new (or existing) skill sets were developed (or enhanced)? What wisdom was gained? What do we now know about this issue, the community, or ourselves that we didn't know before?
Celebrating	Celebrate moments, teamwork, starting, finishing, achieving, growing, and learning.
Continuing the cycle	What does what we did mean for us now? Where's our next effort for change? Do we continue a particular project and take it deeper? explore a different angle that popped up? tackle a root cause we've exposed? try something new? What concerns do we see now? How do we get ready for our next undertaking? What do we need to do?

READY-TO-GO SERVICE PROJECTS

Making the Move From Service to Service-learning

Now that you know the basics of service-learning, this question remains: What does it take to move from service to service-learning?

Consider this typical experience of a youth group in Anytown, USA, that is working with a local mission in their soup kitchen.

> The group served food at a local soup kitchen on a regular basis. The group's youth pastor decided that a time of reflection was necessary so that the youth could process what they were doing and grow in compassion and understanding.
>
> Before going to the soup kitchen (pre-reflection), the youth pastor asked the group what they thought about going to the soup kitchen and what the experience would be like.
>
> The youth gave answers such as, "I think the homeless are people who don't have motivation" and "They're all crazy or lazy."
>
> The group went in and took up their positions, standing behind the counter and serving food and drinks; they carried platters to the tables and refilled drinks as needed. They did their assigned tasks and little else.
>
> After the service project was done, the youth pastor gathered the youth together, eager to see how attitudes had changed. She asked, "What do you think, now that you have spent time with the homeless?" The results were disappointing. Nothing had changed in their attitudes about those they served. They still thought they were lazy, crazy, and unmotivated.

Let's step back and look at the story. It reflects a common service experience: Go in, do the task, and leave. It also reflects a common first experience when a youth pastor tries to add a little piece of service-learning to deepen the experience.

Some youth pastors at this point may give up and say, "Service-learning doesn't work. I've tried it. I've done reflection, and the service experience just hasn't changed the teens' biases and attitudes."

How can you more deeply engage the youth and have a greater impact? See what this youth pastor did:

> She recognized immediately that what the youth group was doing was only perpetuating their attitudes about homelessness. She recognized that the youth were not mingling and interacting with the homeless in a meaningful way.

> The leader then decided to incorporate an interview into the overall experience. Before the next time at the soup kitchen, she gave the group an assignment: During lunch, each youth would take a break at different times, have lunch with some of the homeless persons, and interview at least one of the lunchmates. The youth were to invite their lunchmates to tell something about their life and history and something about their hopes.

> At the end of their time, the group came back together and the leader asked them what they had learned. The youth told the stories they had heard. They'd learned that homelessness is not just the result of succumbing to addictions or mental illness. Some of these persons had had successful lives and families until a business closed down, jobs were lost, family members got sick, and the medical expenses were more than they could afford.

> The teens reached a new level of understanding and compassion. The homeless persons they were serving were simply people who'd fallen on hard times. Homelessness could happen to anyone.

By adding the relational factor, the youth pastor created an opportunity for compassion and connections to take root.

While not yet leading a full service-learning experience, the youth pastor took first steps: weaving in reflection time on the front end, during the project (as they did interviews), and at the end. She provided time, space, and opportunity for learning to take place. She also removed the barriers of "us versus them" so that it simply became "us."

Her brilliance was not simply to have interview questions that addressed the needs and situations of the people but also to include a question to get at their hopes and aspirations. She put a human face on a social issue and helped the youth realize that homeless people are human beings who deserve love, acceptance, and respect.

She also empowered the youth group to go out and find for themselves what the real deal was. She pushed them to develop their skills and explore an issue unfamiliar to them instead of simply accepting things at face value. Her steps were a good start for turning a service experience into something more lasting and valuable.

That story is one example of taking an existing service project and introducing elements of service-learning. Here is another way:

From Service to Service-learning: a Sample Process

→ Start with food. (This part is a no-brainer.)

→ Gather the group together, eat, and pose a question for conversation: What do you think about (name of issue)?

→ Sit back and listen. Let them openly discuss the issue. Don't rush into the conversation to give your own opinion. Let them chew on it.

→ Interject questions when they're needed to keep the conversation going: Is (name of issue) an important issue for teenagers? for our community? Why, or why not? If you decide that this issue is relevant, what could you do to address it?

→ As the youth talk about the issue and what they could do, take notes.

→ If the youth have a passion and concern for the issue, ask the group members what they want to do about it. Ask whether they need to talk with certain people or agencies to check their assumptions before taking action.

→ Begin collecting information, developing a plan, and recruiting others to join the effort. Then take action.

→ Finally, review what you've done and see what other ideas bubble up.

What Does It Take to Move From Service to Service-learning?

We asked this question of various youth workers and pastors across the country who are leading dynamic service-learning programs. These core principles came up time after time:

1. Keep it real.

Find out what the real needs are in the community. Ask your youth. Ask people in the community. Find out what is important to these people and how you can address these issues and injustices.

A true service-learning experience cannot be organized solely by a single authority figure or even a small leadership team. No single person has the complete picture of what is going on in our world. To fully understand the issues we wish to address, we have to enter other people's worlds and seek to understand their experiences, their perspectives, and even their history. Only when we enter their world will true compassion and understanding take root.

2. Give away power.

"Youth are informed all day by teachers. They are told what to do by their parents. They naturally defer their power to adults," explains Anderson, an inner-city youth worker in low-income neighborhoods. "To give away power takes incredible awareness on the part of the adult working with the youth group. We are in a position to teach them to claim their own power and to not be so quick to defer it."

Give away power whenever and wherever possible: Youth should select, design, implement, and even evaluate their service project. They should take ownership of the project from start to finish. If a youth asks what a word means, instead of answering tell that youth to look it up. Let the youth learn for themselves. As the project progresses, try to give away more and more power until the youth are running things and you are just the sounding board and advisor. Help them realize that they have power to do things on their own, to use their own abilities to find solutions to problems.

Part of helping them use their own brains is to question stereotypes when they come into the picture. The adult leader should listen for these stereotypes, not to attack them but to interject and question the youth when stereotypes arise. "What do you mean by that? Where did you develop that idea or attitude?" If youth are to learn from the service experience, the leader must be careful not to impose his or her own knowledge but simply to ask questions and challenge the group to go deeper.

Giving away power is countercultural, especially in adult-youth relationships, and will take discipline. But giving power to your youth is essential if you are to make the move from service to service-learning. Youth learn most effectively when they have the opportunity to ask questions, when they must work together to make decisions, and when they are challenged to use their gifts and abilities in new ways.

In the movie *Bruce Almighty*, God (played by Morgan Freeman) says to Bruce (played by Jim Carrey), "People want me to do everything for them. What they don't realize is that they have the power. You want to see a miracle? Be the miracle."

3. Be intentional.

Set the tone from the beginning that the group is going to learn by doing, by relating, and by inward examination. Be intentional in empowering youth and in providing opportunities for youth to learn about themselves and others. Be intentional in involving the community throughout planning, doing, and reflecting so that relationships develop and preconceived misconceptions are exposed and debunked. Be intentional in including youth with disabilities or who do not have English as their first language. Incorporate all the youth in your church or neighborhood into your program—be intentional about not overlooking and excluding anyone.

> "We must, indeed, all hang together or, most assuredly, we shall all hang separately."
>
> (attributed to Benjamin Franklin)

4. Enact and promote working *with*.

Too often, youth ministers plan a service project *for* their youth so that they can do something *for* the community. Service-learning is different: We organize a project *with* our youth and *with* members of the community so that the youth can work *with* one another and the community.

Service-learning equalizes the playing field; it breaks through the superficial "haves" and "have-nots" barrier (that is, privileged vs. poor, healthy vs. dealing with health challenges, and so on) to reveal the truth that every

"Service-learning shows that we're in this together. My issues or struggle is not mine alone. It's part of a bigger tapestry. No one is alone. No issue is simple or solitary. The first answer is usually the wrong answer. Service-learning can put youths' crisis within a more truthful context for their lives, and it is liberating for them to know they're not alone in their struggle. They can then claim power and liberation to act in truth and shared responsibility for justice, because they are freed from illusion and know the truth of what's really going on in the world. They then know how they can act."

—Anderson, youth worker

person is a gift of experiences, knowledge, and abilities. Everyone has something to contribute and is capable of naming the injustices in society and doing something about them.

Believing that every person is a valuable resource who can contribute requires openness and shared power instead of passing on one's own agenda. Taking on this attitude means saying, "You know things I don't know. You have this wealth of knowledge that I don't have," acknowledging that people with different ages and life experiences are needed to successfully tackle the given problem.

5. Encourage introspection.

Going inward allows us to examine our thoughts, beliefs, and values, and how our behaviors reflect them. Understanding who we are and what is important to us gives us the courage and confidence to act in ways that are consistent with our values and beliefs. Take time to know yourself and be true to yourself, as you grow in leadership!

Question, question, question! Take the Socratic approach and question everything. Encourage the youth to make connections between the issues they're addressing, their life experience, and their values. Encourage reflection as a practice of spiritual discipline and development.

As you saw in the example of the group serving at the homeless shelter, if we don't allow time for questioning and introspection, old prejudices and stereotypes will persist. Questioning and reflection are necessary if transformation is to take place.

READY-TO-GO SERVICE PROJECTS

Part 2: Readying Your Hands

Use these activities to get things going and open your group's eyes to community needs, identify group and individual strengths, and plan ways to serve the community. Each session includes reflective conversation starters and activities to help gear the youth up for service.

AN INTRO TO SERVICE-LEARNING

Everything works better when you include food, especially when you are working with youth. In explaining service-learning to your youth group, have a make-your-own-banana-split social to help illustrate the point.

Holding your own banana split, deliver this monologue to the youth:

> Think about a banana split. The boat that holds this delectable treat represents preparation or organization, because it holds everything together. If there is no organization in place, things may fall apart or melt away.

> The banana is sliced in two. One half represents service and action; the other half, reflection and learning. The two halves make up the whole; both are needed for a great banana split and for a great service-learning experience.

> The vanilla, strawberry, and chocolate ice cream scoops represent the diversity of goals, talents, personalities, and dreams within your group. Each member of the group has his or her own unique "flavor."

> The hot fudge syrup on top is pure celebration. What service-learning experience is complete without celebrating what we have accomplished, learned, and contributed?

> Mix in a few nuts for fun on top of the banana split, and you have the perfect banana split! What banana split is complete without fun and toppings?

> These key ingredients make up service-learning. How well your project turns out depends in great part on your consistency and the amounts of each ingredient you mix in.

> If you leave the banana out, for example, you no longer have a banana split but only ice cream. Likewise, if you leave out intentional reflection, you have only a service project. If you use one type of ice cream, your banana split will be bland. Likewise, if you rely on only a few youth for their leadership or talents, you will lose the richness of what others can offer. In both cases, your final result will fall short of what you were hoping to create: a memorable, delectable, rich experience.

EXPERIENCES WITH SERVICE

Think About It

As you prepare for this activity, think about what your experience with service has been.

Talk About It

Ask:

➜ When have you been part of a service project that was really fun or meaningful? If so, what was it?

➜ What made that experience stand out for you?

➜ If you haven't done a service project yet, what is something you've always wanted to do or help out with? What is an issue you are concerned about and would like to address? How do you want to make the world a better place?

Do Something With It

Supplies: magazines, glue sticks, scissors, markers, posterboard or chart paper

Create a collage of ways in which the members of your group want to make the world a better place. (Or create a collage that represents the fun and meaningful service projects that the youth have done in the past.)

Reflect on It

Ask:

➜ What do our combined experiences, hopes, and dreams tell us about what we can do if we work together?

Celebrate It

Hang your collage in the youth group area or around the church. You could also take a digital picture to post on your youth group website. The images will inspire the group to serve others in the youth group, the church, and the larger community.

EXPLORING THE MEANING OF SERVICE

Think About It

Reflect on these questions as you prepare for this activity:

→ What does serving mean?

→ What other words do we use interchangeably with the word *service*?

Talk About It

Ask:

→ What's the value of serving?

→ When we set out to serve our neighbors and community, how do we benefit? How do others benefit?

→ Sharon, a youth worker from New York says, "Christians should come to see service as a part of who we are. Just our everyday living. Not an obligation. Not getting any compensation. We just do it." What do you think about this quotation? How does it shape your understanding of service?

Do Something With It

Supplies: notecards or slips of paper, dictionary, sheet of paper, pencils, posterboard

Have the youth write their own definition of *service* on an index card or slip of paper, and tell them to put their initials at the top. Record a dictionary definition on an index card or slip of paper as well. Collect all the definitions, mix them up, and read them aloud one at a time. Ask the youth to vote for the one definition they think is the actual dictionary version. Award a person one point for each vote his or her definition gets. (For instance, if three people think Eric's definition is the dictionary version, then Eric gets three points.) At the end, tally up the number of votes for each definition. Award anyone who correctly guesses the dictionary version five points (in addition to any votes his or her definition receives). Give high fives or a round of applause for the highest score and correct guesses.

Put all the definitions side by side, and have your group meld them together to create your youth group's definition of *service*. Talk about the differences and similarities among their individual definitions, the dictionary's definition, and their perceptions of what service means. How, if at all, has the concept of service changed throughout the years? How vital was it in biblical days? How vital is it now?

Ask the students to look up **Acts 6:1-6,** and have a volunteer read aloud this Scripture. Tell the youth that this dispute about widows was one of the first real conflicts the Christian community faced. The Greek widows were complaining because the Jewish widows were getting preferential treatment. Seven deacons were selected to serve all the widows and make sure that they got food and whatever they needed.

Point out that widows (members of the community) brought up the need. Seven people were selected to oversee efforts to meet the need. These deacons took care of their assigned tasks, but they also took leadership roles in other ways, preaching and interpreting Scripture. What happened with the deacons and the apostles is often true for those of us who serve today. Service-learning opens up eyes. We may start with one task that addresses one issue; but then we may get involved with other efforts to meet other needs.

After the group has agreed on a definition of *service,* have someone write the definition on posterboard or large sheet of paper. Hang it in a visible place as a reminder of the importance of service. If time permits, invite the youth to come up with a pledge to be servant leaders, to write the pledge on the posterboard, and to sign their names to it.

Reflect on It

Read **Micah 6:8b** (NIV): "And what does the Lord require of you? To act justly and to love mercy and to walk humbly with your God."

Ask:

→ Whom do you know who does the right thing and acts justly? Whom do you know who shows kindness and mercy toward others?

Celebrate It

Supplies: thank-you cards and pens

Ask the youth to send a thank-you note to someone in their life who truly exemplifies service. The person might be a pastor, a parent, teacher, neighbor, or friend. Celebrating and honoring people who sacrifice to make a difference in the community is important.

THE POWER TO MAKE A DIFFERENCE

Think About It

Martin Luther King, Jr. said that anyone can be great because anyone can serve.

Talk About It

Tell the youth that Sharon, a youth worker, has posted King's saying (above) in her office so that she can look at it every day. She says she wants to remind herself that being great is simply a matter of helping others any way she can. It doesn't matter whether she gives clothes that no longer fit her to the girl next door or opens a door for someone whose hands are full or walks the neighbors' dog while they're out of town or brings in a meal when someone's sick. She can do things for others every day, and that way of life makes her truly great. She can be great, and you can be great every day.

Ask:

➜ Do you agree with Sharon and Martin Luther King, Jr. that to truly be great all one has to do is serve others? Why, or why not?

➜ How do friends and peers, the media, and society as a whole shape our view of what greatness is?

Read **Matthew 25:31-40*** and **Mark 9:33-37.** Then ask:

➜ What do these passages say about the relationship between greatness and serving others?

➜ According to **Matthew 25:35-36,** what are some practical ways in which we can give of ourselves and serve others?

➜ What are the fruits or the consequences of our service?

➜ How does Jesus' teaching in **Mark 9:33-37** conflict with our culture's understanding of greatness?

Read **Matthew 20:16; 22:34-40; Mark 10:35-45; Romans 13:8-10;** and **Galatians 5:13-14.** Then ask:

➜ What is the overarching message of these Scriptures? How do they apply to service-learning?

46

➜ What motivation do we have for service?

➜ What do these verses tell us about the relationship between loving and serving our neighbors and loving God?

Point out that these Scriptures call us to a life of love and service, not just to one-time acts of kindness.

Look at **Matthew 20:16** a little more closely. This verse deals with equality, showing that God loves all persons equally, regardless of any power or economic advantages that one person has over another. All of us are God's children, and God loves us all. Thus we should think of everyone we work with on a service project as our equals and treat them with love and grace.

Read **Matthew 20:1-15.**

The landowner hires folks and pays them all the same, regardless of when they started working. It tells us that God's grace is sufficient for all of us. We can't earn more than God's grace even if we work all day.

Note: If anyone asks, "Why do service?" refer them to **Matthew 25:31-40.** When doing these acts of compassion and justice, we are being Jesus for the world and making his kingdom real here on earth.

Do Something With It

Dr. King's words echo these Scriptures. Challenge the youth to create their own statement based on these Scriptures to inspire people to serve. Give the youth ten minutes to create new inspirations.

Challenge the group to look for opportunities to do acts of service each day in the coming week. Have them keep a journal of what they do each day and review what they did at your next meeting.

Reflect on It

What other quotations or sayings inspire you? Ask the youth to bring their favorite quotations to the next meeting.

Celebrate It

Supplies: strip of cloth or canvas, markers, basket

The following week, talk about the acts of service that the youth have done, asking about how the students felt about it.

Then ask each person to use a permanent marker to write a favorite quotation on a strip of cloth or canvas. Collect all the strips in a basket, and pass the basket around the circle, inviting each person to pick a random strip of canvas. Ask each person to read aloud the one they chose.

Close the activity by inviting everyone to take their new inspiration home to keep in a special place they can look at each day to inspire them to greatness and service.

"Teenagers enjoy knowing they have helped someone else. They are so accustomed to hearing negative comments about themselves. They so often live in the face of assumptions that they will never do anything or be anybody. Service makes them feel good about themselves. It's a big deal!"

—Ingrid, youth worker

UNITING IN PURPOSE

Think About It

God arranged the members in the body, each one of them, as [God] chose. If all were a single member, where would the body be? As it is, there are many members, yet one body.... If one member suffers, all suffer together with it; if one member is honored, all rejoice together with it.

—**1 Corinthians 12:18-20, 26**

Talk About It

Ask someone to read aloud the Scripture. Ask another volunteer to look up and read aloud **1 Corinthians 12:12, 14-27.**

Ask the group:

➜ What is the core message of this Scripture?

➜ What power is there in being one of purpose?

Do Something With It (Option 1)

Have the group break into pairs or groups of three.

➜ Round 1: Determine something that you all have in common (such as being vegetarian or running track).

➜ Round 2: Talk about about a skill you bring to the group (such as first-aid training, a passion for project planning, or an ability to write well).

➜ Round 3: Talk about about something that gives your meaning and purpose to your life (such as family, love of God, or teaching others to read).

➜ Round 4: Talk about what you would change about the world to make it a better place.

After the activity, ask the group:

➜ This game is about connections. Why are connections important?

Then go over the following points:

➜ Round one was about commonalities: When we spend time and get to know others, we often find we have some sort of common bond.

→ Round two was about skills and talents: Our skills and talents meet needs and fill in gaps; we don't all have the same skills and talents. An awareness of each person's gifts helps us work together more effectively.

→ Round three was about purpose and meaning: When we show people what makes our lives meaningful, we encourage them to look for meaning and purpose in their own life.

→ Round four was about vision: A clear vision of how we want to change the world and the difference we want to make unites like-minded people and provides the "umph" that will enable us to work together toward a common cause. Our vision is the glue that holds together our diverse group of people.

Then ask:

→ What did we discover about what we have in common and the skills and talents this group has?

→ What sorts of things give your friends a sense of meaning and purpose?

→ What difference did people in your group say they wanted to make in the community?

→ How were your partners' visions similar to or different from yours?

→ How can we find a common vision and purpose for our group—one that lets each of us to give from the best of who we are to the common good?

As time permits, have the group come up with a mission statement for the group. Record this statement, along with their definition of *service* on a posterboard; hang it on the wall of your meeting space.

Do Something With It (Option 2)

Supplies: DVD or VCR player, TV monitor and a copy of the movie Drumline*

Show these clips from the movie *Drumline*:

→ Devon doesn't wake his roommate up, and Doctor Lee goes over the band motto with the group; as a result, the band works together.

→ Devon and his section leader, Sean, face off over differences and settle them in the recording room; they work together, presenting ideas to Dr. Lee of a combo of old and new music.

→ The top two bands' drumlines face off at the end.

Point out the band's "one band, one sound" motto. Ask:

→ What do you think of the motto?

→ How does this motto reinforce the message from Scripture?

→ How did the clips from the movie reinforce the importance of honoring one another's gifts or overcoming differences to work together?

→ What was the payoff of working together and putting the common good over self?

Reflect on It

Remind the youth of these two points:

→ Each of us has something we can contribute to the group.

→ When we work together, we accomplish more than we do working alone.

Ask the youth to think about what they value about what each person brings to the group and to keep these things in mind while working together.

Celebrate It

Supplies: sheets of paper, masking tape, and markers

Give each person a sheet of paper to put on his or her back with masking tape; also give each youth a marker. Have the youth mingle and write on the backs of each person (on the sheet of paper) one thing they value about that person, whether it is a talent or an ability or a personality trait.

When all are done, have each person take off his or her sheet of paper and receive the gift of appreciation from the rest of the group.

*When you show home videocassettes or DVDs to a group of learners, you need to obtain a license. You can get a public performance license from Christian Video Licensing International (1-888-771-2854, *cvli.com*). The license can cost over $100. Check with your church to see whether an umbrella license has already been obtained. Through conferences, jurisdictions, dioceses, and other structures, many denominations secure licenses for their churches to show films.

EXPERIENCES IN SERVANT LEADERSHIP

Think About It

The 2002–2003 National Study of Youth and Religion found that 32 percent of youth reported "regularly or occasionally" doing "volunteer work or community service . . . (not counting required service . . . by school, juvenile justice program)."

Talk About It

Would you say that you regularly or occasionally perform acts of service? Do your friends regularly or occasionally do volunteer work or community service?

Do Something With It

Supplies: Servant Leadership Triangle handouts and pens

Hand out copies of the Servant Leadership Triangle handout from page 170. Point out that the triangle is divided into four levels. Tell the youth to fill out those triangles by following these instructions:

➔ In the top level, write the qualities of a good servant leader.

➔ In the second level, write ways you've served in your home, your school, your church, or your community. Examples include baking cookies for a new neighbor, picking up trash around campus, painting a room for an elderly friend, or tutoring a child.

➔ In the third level, write leadership roles that you've played in the past. Examples might include teaching a child to tie a shoe, handing out bulletins at church, teaching a Sunday school class, or being the treasurer of a club at school.

➔ In the bottom level, write three skills or talents that you could use as a servant leader.

➔ Write your name beneath the triangle.

Reflect on It

Ask:

→ Are you satisfied with the amount of time you spend serving others? How could you make more time for service?

→ What would help pull more youth into service? What would engage them and entice them to be more involved?

Break the group into teams of two or three, and ask each group to create an ad campaign to sell the idea of service to their friends and peers. Give the teams several minutes to work; then have each team present its creation.

Celebrate It

Celebrate all the ways your youth, either as a group or as individuals, have given of themselves to the community.

Collect from the group their Servant Leadership Triangle handouts, and read aloud some of the ways your youth have been servant leaders. Tell the youth that if an item you read applies to them, they should jump from their seats and yell out, "That's me!" Try to end this session by naming something that you know would apply to all of your youth, so that all of the participants can claim their servanthood and rejoice.

CREATING OPPORTUNITIES FOR SERVICE

Think About It

In a 2002 survey conducted on youth-adult relationships, 52% of adults said they thought it was "most important" to model giving and serving for youth, while 56% said that they themselves set an example for young people of giving and serving.*

Talk About It

Read aloud the statement above. Ask:

→ What do you think about that statement?

→ How do the adults in your life (at church, at school, in clubs, and so on) model service or provide service opportunities?

→ What persons or agencies do you know of that give young people opportunities to serve?

→ What could the adults in your lives (as well as schools, churches, and other organizations) do better?

→ What opportunities would you like to have that aren't currently provided?

→ How could you create more service opportunities for you and your peers?

Do Something With It

Play the Resources Game, the Connect-the-Dots Game, or both.

Resources Game: This game identifies the resources we have for serving and shows the importance of working together and using our resources wisely.

Supplies: notecards, markers, masking tape, 10 pieces of cardboard, marker

Set down two strips of masking tape 25 feet apart to mark the boundaries.

First ask the youth to identify a service project they are thinking about. Then have the group choose one of two boundary lines and line up behind it.

Ask the youth to identify what resources might help them on their service project. (Examples include church members, space at church, youth group volunteers, their mom's catering friend, and the local hardware store.)

Write down ten of the resources they name on the cardboard squares (one resource per square), and give them the ten squares. Tell them that the floor space between the two boundaries represents the obstacles that make service difficult (such as illness, supplies that don't come through, and bad weather). Explain that project success lies just past the far boundary. The team's mission is to use their "resources" to get through the "obstacles" to the other side, which represents success in their service.

Explain the following parameters:

➔ They must get everyone across the "obstacles" and to the other boundary by touching only the ten "resources" (cardboard squares).

➔ They must keep in contact with the resources at all times. If at any point at least one person is not touching one of the resources, that resources is no longer available. (Obviously, they didn't need it, anyway.)

➔ If someone steps off the resources into the "obstacles," then the group loses one of its resources.

➔ The team should take as many of the resources as possible to so that the youth can still use them after the group's success.

After answering questions for clarification, let the youth go at it. When they've finished, have them count the resources they were able to keep. Ask:

➔ Were you successful? Why?

➔ How did you, individually and as a group, deal with losing a resource?

➔ How many of the resources did you use?

➔ How did being able to see the finish line motivate you?

Make the connection between the game and real life by asking:

➔ What resources are important for us to succeed in our service project?

➔ Why is keeping contact with our resources important? What happens when we don't make use of these resources?

➔ How do we stay motivated in situations where we may not see the fruits of our labor for a long time?

➔ How is this game an analogy both for doing service and for relating to others? (The group actively worked together toward success and were expected to tend to one another and the resources at hand.)

Connect-the-Dots Game: If your group has a service project in mind, this game will help the youth identify the resources needed, who already has connections, and where connections need to be made.

Supplies: markers, sticky notes that are at least 3" x 3"

Play connect the dots. Write the word *today* on a sticky note, and place it on the wall. On a second sticky note, write the name of the service project or issue you want to tackle. Place the second note about two feet to the right of the first one. Ask the group to help you connect the dots by filling in the resources and relationships that you need to accomplish your mission, writing specific people, groups, individuals, agencies, and other resources on each sticky note. After you have connected those dots, make a note of which resources are already available and which relationships have already been established. Then look for resources that you need to obtain and relationships that you need to initiate. Ask for volunteers who will take the initiative to seek out these resources and relationships.

Reflect on It

Mohandas Gandhi said, "We must be the change we wish to see in the world."

Ask:

→ How are you a resource for change? What can you do regardless of whether others around you are living out their call to serve others?

Celebrate It

Create or print off certificates of acknowledgement for some of the people and groups that the youth identified earlier (in "Do Something With It") as resources for serving. If you are creating the certificates by hand, write or draw images that reflect the various ways these people or agencies have enabled young people to make a difference in the community. If you are printing them off, a simple "in recognition of your support in enabling youth leadership and service" will suffice. Have all of your youth sign the certificates. Then frame and present the certificates.

Use this time to encourage internal recognition as well. Let the youth acknowledge and recognize one another and how each person has stepped up and served others.

* Grading Grown-Ups 2002: How Do American Kids and Adults Relate? A National Study.
Search Institute © 2003.

ISSUES WE CARE ABOUT

Think About It

Remind the youth that service-learning involves service *and* reflection on what happened and what you've learn from the experience.

Talk About It

Supplies: copies of the service-learning continuum from page 171, pens or pencils, ten sheets of scrap paper, tape, a marker

Hand out copies of the Service-Learning Continuum from page 171.

Ask each youth to rank each item in order from service to service-learning by placing the item that represents the highest level of service-learning at the top and the item that most represents service *without* learning at the bottom. The other eight items should be ranked accordingly. The ten items are:

→ Tutoring a student who is struggling in math

→ Sponsoring an exchange student from another country

→ Reading the newspaper

→ Making a peanut-butter-and-jelly sandwich for your little sister

→ Giving blood

→ Building houses for families in need during spring break

→ Visiting a resident of a nursing home

→ Talking to others about service

→ Serving dinner to the homeless

→ Organizing a group to protest a decision to locate a landfill near a residential area

→ Teaching financial-literacy courses for persons who don't know how to manage their money

As the youth are working, tape ten sheets of scrap paper in a line on the floor, and indicate which sheet represents the top of the continuum and which represents the bottom. When the youth are done working, read aloud one of the examples from above, and ask each person to move to the space that reflects how he or she rated that item. Ask the youth to talk about how they came to conclusions about ranking the examples. Emphasize that there is no correct order and that each person defines *service-learning* differently, based on how they perceive what takes place.

"It's not *what* the action is; it's how it's packaged with youth roles of leadership, reflection, and celebration. Service-learning can be a daily occurrence in our lives if we add intentionality of introspection, digging deeper to examine causes, then taking action."

—Anderson, youth worker

Note that the difference between service and service-learning comes down to reflection. With proper reflection, any of the items could be service-learning activities.

Look at the activities that got the lowest rankings. Discuss how could the group could turn those activities into service-learning.

Do Something With It*

Supplies: newspapers, paper, pens

Give each person a section of newspaper. Ask each participant to find something of interest to him or her in the given section of the paper—an article, an advertisement, or something else.

Then divide the youth into pairs or groups of three and have the youth talk in their groups about what they selected. Ask the groups to find some connection among the items each member of the group found. Then challenge each group to combine these items into a single service experience.

This activity is designed to challenge the group to think non-traditionally about creating action plans and to realize the importance of pulling together the various passions of the people who will be involved in doing service.

Option: Have the students read their newspaper sections and find a story about an issue that catches their attention, something they are passionate about, or an item that portrays an injustice that bothers them. In pairs, the youth should talk about what caught their attention and why. Then the two persons in each pair should:

➔ identify a need connected to the two issues they've selected;

➔ determine what they hope to accomplish and learn; and

➔ design an action plan to address the need that includes whom they might pull in as resources.

Give them time to work; then ask each pair to present its ideas to the others.

Reflect on It

Ask:

→ Which of the issues or injustices that you read about or that others raised really get you riled up? Which ones make you angry, frustrated, or sad?

→ What do you want to do about these issues or injustices?

Challenge the group in the coming week to watch and read the news and tune in to what people are talking about at the dinner table, at school, in church, and around the neighborhood. Tell them to pay attention to ways God may be calling them to tackle injustices around them.

The following week, check in to see what the youth have learned about their world, the pressing issues that affect them, and ideas they have for how to respond to these issues in loving action.

Celebrate It

Supplies: table, puzzle that has as many pieces as you have group members (but not many more pieces than you have group members)

Give each person a puzzle piece. Have the youth mill around until two people can finally fit their pieces together. When a pair of youth have joined these first two pieces together, ask the pair to set these pieces on the table. As other pairs of youth link their pieces together, ask them to see whether their pieces fit with the ones already on the table. If not, have the pair lay down its two pieces on the table and wait for further linkage opportunities.

After the puzzle is put together, talk about how all the pieces are needed for the picture to come into focus. This game illustrates that in community work, we need all the pieces—each person's knowledge, passions, and experience—to come together before we can fully understand the work we're doing.

Thanks to Tony Ganger, who has over two decades of youth-work experience from West Virginia to Ohio to Illinois to California, for sharing this activity with us.

 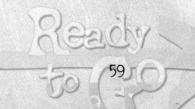

LEADERSHIP: IT'S ALL ABOUT US

Think About It

Jesus was a master service-learning teacher. He knew the members of his team and the gifts they had; he modeled the importance of getting to know persons in the community and tapping into their resources. Consider the miraculous feedings in which he multiplied the little food provided by people in the crowd and fed thousands (**Mark 6:30-44; 8:1-10**). Jesus constantly met real needs and made sure his disciples were paying attention. He would take them aside afterward and explain things to make sure that they got the point.

Have you ever noticed all the times Jesus did something wonderful then turned to his disciples and asked, "What did I just do?"

Ask the group to name some of the stories they know in the Bible where Jesus involved the community as resources to meet the problems they faced.

Talk About It

Have volunteers read aloud **Mark 6:30-44** (the feeding of the five thousand). Then ask:

→ What was the obvious need? *(food)*

→ Who were the ones trying to do service and help others? *(Jesus' disciples)*

→ Who was being served? *(the community, the people)*

→ What plan did the disciples have to meet the need? *("Send them away so that they may . . . buy something for themselves to eat" [**Mark 6:36**].)*

→ What resources did the disciples forget about? *(The people! They forgot to work with those whom they wanted to serve, who knew more about the resources on hand.)*

→ What plan did Jesus offer? *(Gather all the food that people had; break the people into smaller groups.)*

→ What was the result of this plan? *(Everyone had enough to eat.)*

→ If Jesus were to turn to his disciples at this point and ask them, "What did you just learn from this experience?" what do you think his disciples would say? *(Serving is not about doing for, it's about doing with; we are one body, and we need to work with other members of the body to create solutions. When a community works together, it can do incredible things.)*

→ What can we learn from this service-learning experience? *(Don't make assumptions about the people you're serving; regard these people as equals and involve them in the process; break big projects into smaller, more manageable projects.)*

Do Something With It (Choose one from below.)

→ Knowing where food comes from and making it last are important. Have the students cultivate a garden and prepare their own meal by using only food from the garden. This activity illustrates how feeding the crowd worked when everyone pitched in what they had.

→ Beforehand, ask the youth to bring a canned food item; then let the group figure out a meal based on what everyone brought.

→ Participate in feeding your city's homeless population. Sort food at a food bank, and help distribute the food to individuals and agencies. Or serve a meal at rescue mission then sit as others serving at the mission feed you.

→ Contact a local place that works with the hungry, and find out what needs they have. Beyond serving meals, some places collect soap, shampoo, and other items to distribute to those in need.

Reflect on It

If you did either of the first two options, say, "One aspect of leadership is tapping into the power of the people around you." Ask:

→ How did we tap into the power of our group in putting together this meal?

If you did the third option, reflect on the experience of serving and then being served at the mission.

If you did the fourth option, ask,

→ In what simple ways can you support others in your community every day?

> "If you have anything extra, you need to give it to someone else. Whatever we have, we give to others."
>
> —Sharon Williams, nineteen-year youth worker

Celebrate It

For the first three options: Eat the meal together in thanks!

LIVING A LIFE OF KINDNESS

Think About It

Supplies: TV, DVD player, the movie Pay It Forward, *film license (described on page 51)*

Show the clip from the movie *Pay It Forward* in which Trevor presents his plan for paying kindness forward as his classroom project.

Talk About It

Ask the youth to tell stories about how someone has shown them kindness. Ask them how they responded to these gestures of kindness.

Then ask:

➜ Why should Christians show kindness to others? Do you think that Christians behave any more kindly than non-Christians? Explain.

> "Share with God's people who are in need. Practice hospitality."
>
> —**Romans 12:13** (NIV)

Do Something With It

Read the picture book *Somebody Loves You, Mr. Hatch,* by Eileen Spinelli.

Or summarize the book by saying: "Mr. Hatch lives an ordinary life, very much to himself, until a mystery package is delivered to his door with an anonymous love note. Wondering who might be his secret admirer, he starts to be nice to everyone around him. When the postman says he delivered the package to the wrong address, Mr. Hatch is devastated until his friends throw a big party in his honor."

Ask:

➜ What is something little that you can do to brighten someone's day at school, at home, or in your neighborhood?

Distribute copies of the "A Month of Kindness" handout (page 172).

Reflect on It

Supplies: candle, match or lighter, candle holder

Light a candle in a dark room; then say: "Jesus said, 'Let your light shine before men, that they may see your good deeds and praise your Father in heaven' " (**Matthew 5:16,** NIV).

Ask the youth to reflect on the following questions:

➜ What does the verse mean to you?

➜ How does this command affirm or change your behavior?

➜ What effect does the candle's light have on a dark room?

Say, "Our lives should have the same effect on our culture."

Pray that God would help you shine your light brightly in your home, school, church, and community.

Celebrate It

Calculate how many people your youth group would affect by paying kindness forward to three people each. How many people would you affect if those three people were kind to three more people? Rejoice in the power of simple actions that can transform the spirit of a community. Encourage the youth to commit to a lifestyle of kindness.

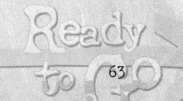

USING YOUR TALENTS

Think About It

What skills and talents do you have? What do you do with them? How do you use your gifts to help others? Do you use your abilities confidently or do they wilt from lack of use?

Talk About It

Read Jesus' parable of the talents from **Matthew 25:14-30.**

To summarize, say: "An employer gave one of his workers five talents, another worker two talents, and a third worker one talent. A talent was a type of money. The man with five talents worked hard, invested his money, and multiplied it so that he had ten talents to give back to his employer. The man with two talents did the same: He invested his money and had four talents to show for his work. Imagine the employer's pleasure with these workers' dedication, work ethic, and productivity.

"But the third man, whether out of fear or laziness, did nothing constructive with his one talent. He merely buried his one talent in the ground and had only that one talent to give to his employer when the employer returned. He had done nothing with what he was given, and his boss was angry."

(Note that although the talents in this story are money, *talent* is an appropriate word because the story also applies to how we use our God-given abilities.)

Say, "The moral of this story is that to whom much is given, much is expected."

Ask the youth to tell stories of how they've used their money, talents, or influence to help others in small or big ways.

Ask the youth whether there have been times when they could have made a difference and didn't—a time when they "buried" their talents. Why were they reluctant to use their gifts?

Say: "In the comic book that features Spider-Man's first appearance, Spider-Man's uncle tells him, 'With great power there must also come great responsibility' " (*Amazing Fantasy #15,* August 1962).

Ask:

➜ How is this quotation about Spider-Man similar to the message of the parable of the talents?

64   **READY-TO-GO SERVICE PROJECTS**

Do Something With It

Supplies: copies of "A Look at You" (page 173) and "You at Your Best" (page 174), pens, paper, magazines, gluesticks, markers, crayons, posterboard for every three youth, gold candy coins

Address the group: "How can we get the greatest return from our talents? First, we need to identify our gifts and abilities. Second, we should celebrate these talents; they're part of what makes each of us unique. Finally, we need to find meaningful ways to use our talents."

Distribute the handouts "A Look at You" and "You at Your Best," and instruct the youth to complete them. These handouts help the youth identify their God-given abilities.

After the students have had time to work, assign them to groups of three. Have each person tell his or her group members three of his or her talents. Someone in the group should write down all of the skills (nine in all) named by the group.

Reflect on It

Have each group use its nine talents to create a poem, skit, story, collage, song, or other artwork that celebrates the gifts it has. The group must use all nine words in its artwork, and everyone must participate in the presentation. (Allow twenty minutes for the groups to create their masterpieces.)

Celebrate It

For fun, consider setting up a coffee house with music and drinks, where the groups can present their creations.

Doing Something More With It

Option 1: Give each person a gold candy coin, and challenge everyone to pick a way to use his or her talents during the next week. Have the youth report back next week about what they did. The coin serves as a reminder to the youth to multiply their talents.

Option 2: Give each youth member $2 or $5 each to multiply during the next two weeks. Brainstorm ways they could multiply their "talents." (Example: Buy a six-pack of soft drinks, and sell them for fifty cents each.) Gather their multiplied "talents," and give them to a charity or ministry of your choice.

Hello My Name Is ...

_____

_____

THE POWER OF KNOWING A PERSON

Think About It

Why is getting to know the people whom we're serving important?

Talk About It

Read aloud **Galatians 3:28:** "There is no longer Jew or Greek, there is no longer slave or free, there is no longer male or female; for all of you are one in Christ Jesus."

Say: "Too often we make assumptions about people, events, or issues based on limited knowledge. For example, we may assume that all people from Mexico like rice and beans simply because we know that rice and beans are served at Mexican restaurants. We may chuckle at a joke about women liking chocolate or how men have to hold the remote control, assuming that these descriptions are universal truths because we know some people who fit the bill. But these stereotypes do not tell us the whole truth.

"Jesus, on the other hand, defied this tendency to make assumptions and label people. He saw people for who they were; and he invites us to do the same, commanding us to love our neighbor as ourselves (**Matthew 22:39**). To love our neighbor, we must know our neighbor."

Do Something With It

Supplies: blank nametags, pen

Play the labeling game.

Mark each nametag with a member of a particular clique or subgroup of the teen world (such as computer geek, pregnant girl, star athlete, class president, school newspaper editor, A student, or cheerleader).

Gather the group. Put one label on each person's forehead without telling him or her what is on the nametag. Tell the youth to mingle and to treat each person in accordance with the identity on his or her forehead.

After five minutes, gather the youth back together and ask each person to guess what type of person he or she was. Correct any wrong guesses.

Ask:

→ How did wearing a label feel?

→ How did the labels affect your interaction with one another?

→ In what ways do we label people in our culture?

→ How can we avoid labeling others? (by spending more time getting to know people for who they are)

→ How can we encourage others not to spread rumors or inaccurate information about people?

Reflect on It

Say, "Our society stereotypes many people by looking at factors such as skin color, economic status, and physical ability."

> "Love from the center of who you are; don't fake it.... Be good friends who love deeply."
>
> —**Romans 12:9-10** (*Message*)

Ask:

→ Why are we so quick to judge others?

→ What makes us think we have the right to put others down?

→ How can you intervene when your friends' words or actions are based on prejudices?

→ Sadly, the church can also be a place of judgment and prejudice. What can you do to combat the stereotypes you hear about other people in the church? What about in the larger community?

Celebrate It

Option 1: Different is just different! Have youth create a list of things that they believe make them unique. Ask each student to read aloud each item on his or her list. The others should raise their hand if an item being read also appears on their list. See how many things were entirely unique and appeared on no one else's list.

Option 2: Create and read a list of statements, and have the youth step forward if the statement applies to them. (Examples include, "I like sushi," "I prefer pizza to hamburgers," "Morning is my best time of the day," and "I sing in the shower.")

OVERCOMING OBSTACLES

Think About It

"Don't let anyone look down on you because you are young, but set an example for believers in speech, in life, in love, in faith and in purity" (**1 Timothy 4:12, NIV**).

Talk About It

Read aloud **1 Samuel 17:31-37.**

Say: "The young person in this story saw the need that challenged his community. He didn't think of his age or lack of experience as limitations. Instead, he knew that he could address the need."

Ask:

→ What is amazing to you about this story?

→ Why, do you think, did the giant not seem like an insurmountable problem to David? What kinds of challenges had he already faced?

→ What persons have believed greatly in your abilities? Has an adult ever given you a chance to do something that other adults didn't want to do? How did getting that opportunity make you feel?

→ When have you known that you had the ability to do something even though others discouraged or "poo-pooed" you? How did you handle the situation?

→ Why, do you think, did King Saul give David a chance? Why, do you think, did David have the confidence to step forward?

→ What gave David his sense of confidence and belief?

→ David wasn't necessarily graceful in response to his brother. How can we respond with grace and love to persons who don't support us as much as we would like?

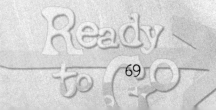

Do Something With It

Follow these steps to do a progressive group stand:

→ Ask everyone to sit down on the floor. Each person should attempt to stand up without using his or her her arms to push off of the floor.

→ Have the youth sit down again. Ask them to do the same thing, but this time start sitting cross legged. (Some may have sat cross legged the first time.)

→ Now have each youth pair off with a youth of similar size. Instruct the partners to stand back-to-back and lock their arms together. Again, ask them to sit down on the floor then stand, this time without unlocking arms.

→ Once a pair has successfully completed the task, ask that pair to join another pair and repeat the task all together. (All youth will have their arms linked and their backs toward one another.)

→ Continue by having groups of four join together and complete the task as a group of eight; but this time, simply have the youth hold hands to prevent potential injury cause by locking arms in large groups.

Continue joining groups together until, eventually, the whole group will be in a circle, attempting to sit down and stand up by supporting one another.

Ask:

→ What obstacles did you face in this activity?

→ How difficult was it to stand by yourself?

→ Was it more difficult to work with a partner? with several partners?

→ What was the key to successfully standing up as a pair or team? (Putting your weight on your partners)

→ What does this activity teach us about working together to overcome obstacles?

→ Sometimes you have to face obstacles alone. When that happens, what strengths can you draw on to overcome such obstacles?

→ Fear is a giant obstacle that often holds people back. What helps you overcome fear?

In the Scripture for this activity, the hero faced a giant. Ask your youth to brainstorm some of "giants" that they and their peers must face. What injustices are going on around them at school or in the community right under their nose? What can they do to confront these giants?

Reflect on It

Read aloud **Deuteronomy 31:6** (NIV): "Be strong and courageous. Do not be afraid or terrified because of them, for the LORD your God goes with you; [God] will never leave you nor forsake you."

Ask:

→ How should the truth in this verse affect the way we live? the way we pursue our dreams? the way we face our fears? the way we serve in the community?

Celebrate It

Ask everyone to sit quietly in a circle on the floor of a quiet room. Explain to the youth that you will initiate a series of actions and that they should copy whatever action the person on their left is doing. Lead the group through the following actions:

→ rubbing hands together

→ snapping fingers

→ slapping knees

→ stomping feet while slapping knees

Continue, leading them through the same actions in reverse, starting with stomping feet while slapping knees and ending with rubbing hands together. Then, as your final action, join hands in prayer. This activity should sound like the coming and going of a rainstorm.

Note to the group that we can make miracles happen when we work together to pursue Kingdom things. Big community change starts with one person's actions and expands until it affects an entire community.

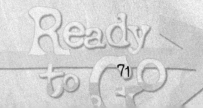

EMBRACING THE INVISIBLE PEOPLE

Think About It

What would it be like to be invisible? Children often have invisible friends and sometimes dream about being invisible. Have you ever noticed that there are people who live with us, go to school with us, go to church with us, or shop in the grocery store with us who go through life practically invisible? Have you ever felt invisible?

Talk About It

Obtain the book *The Red Suit Diaries,* by Ed Butchart (© 2003 by Ed Butchart, published by Fleming H. Revell; available at *www.cokesbury.com*).

Read these excerpts about the various children and adults Santa encountered in his mall visits:

→ "Touched by an Angel": the story of invisible adult sister whom Santa reached out to in love (pages 131–134)

→ "The Child That Stays With You": the story about a severely disabled four-year-old boy who survived drowning (pages 134–139)

→ "Lindsey Brown": the story of a little girl with multiple disabilities who before had been rejected by one Santa (pages 139–144)

→ "James Franklin King": the story about a boy with a misdiagnosed condition whom Santa and his wife were able to embrace (pages 146–153)

Then say, "Many people who face challenges go virtually unnoticed, even though they are around us every day."

Ask:

→ Why, do you think, are some persons invisible to others?

→ In what ways are persons with certain physical, intellectual, or emotional challenges ignored or unnoticed?

→ What, physical, intellectual, or emotional capabilities do you have that you take for granted? What would life be like if you didn't have these abilities?

Do Something With It

Supplies: balloons, blindfolds, wheelchairs, crutches, balls that have a bell or some noisemaker in them, popcorn, craft supplies (such as scissors, glue, glitter, pipe cleaners, construction paper, crayons, popsicle sticks, and tape)

Give the teens opportunities to experience what it is like to live with a physical challenge. Besides temporarily experiencing a certain physical handicap, the youth will get a sense of the emotional challenges that go hand-in-hand with this difficulty.

Assign the youth various roles. One or more youth could be in a wheelchair, some could wear blindfolds, some could be instructed to use one hand, one or more could be on crutches, and others should simply be themselves. Discuss the participants' new abilities and any safety rules pertinent to the series of activities below.

Begin by giving the youth, except the person in the wheelchair, hugs and warm, personal greetings. For the person in the wheelchair, simply pat him or her on the back with a smile and say, "Hi."

Then designate a table for all of the youth to run to and tag. Award a prize (such as a soft drink or small snack) to the first persons to get there. You might also award prizes to the top three or top five finishers. Those who arrive last get nothing. (Those youth who are blindfolded, on crutches, or in a wheelchair likely will arrive last.)

For the next activity, give each youth a balloon and challenge them to bat their balloon in the air and keep it afloat. Award a prize to the person who keeps his or her balloon in the air the longest. (This game disadvantages one-handed persons, as well as those who are blindfolded or on crutches.)

Then have the youth pair off. Instruct the pairs to roll a ball back and forth between them. Use balls that have a bell or other noisemaker inside. Each person will roll the ball as quickly as possible, attempting to roll it past his or her partner. The partner will attempt to catch the ball and roll it back. Each time a player successfully rolls the ball past his or her partner, that player scores a point. The first player to score five points wins. Play several rounds, having the youth switch partners each time. (This activity allows those who are blindfolded to rely on their sense of hearing and creates additional difficulty for persons in a wheelchair.)

Next, create an obstacle course within the room for people to navigate. If you want, designate a few people to help advise the participants on how to navigate the course.

For the last two rounds, have all the youth shed their disadvantages and take off their shoes. Tell the youth to put a few pieces of unpopped popcorn in each shoe and to put their shoes back on. Have them walk laps back and forth across the room as quickly as they can for two minutes. Tell them that this activity represents becoming older, which happens to all of us. With age often comes aches and pains that we can't control, such as aching feet.

Finally, have the group sit in teams of two to six. Distribute craft supplies (such as scissors, glue, glitter, pipe cleaners, construction paper, crayons, popsicle sticks, and tape). Ask the youth to put their dominant hands in their back pockets. As a team, they should work together to create a zoo (or whatever you want them to create) in ten minutes without using their dominant hands. Anyone who cheats by using a dominant hand disqualifies the team. After ten minutes, allow each team to show off its handiwork. This exercise allows the team to experience the challenge that comes with "fumble fingers" and hands that don't work quite as well as they once did—another symptom of aging.

Reflect on It

→ What was completing tasks with additional challenges like?

→ What emotions did you experience during these exercises?

→ What might life be like if you had to face these challenges every day?

→ What have you learned from this experience that you will take with you?

→ How can you be more aware of invisible persons around you and extend welcome and hospitality to them?

→ Besides physical difficulties, what other factors might make persons in our community invisible?

→ How can you better understand what these invisible persons go through?

Celebrate It

Supplies: a geode, one glass stone per youth (such as those sold at craft stores)

Say, "The invisible people we're talking about are people whom our society generally does not value."

Show the outside shell of a geode, and say: "At first glance, this rock doesn't seem like much. Much like we do with invisible people, we might look past this rock or discard it as something having little worth. But God knows better."

Show the crystal formations on the inside of the geode, and say: "God sees through the outer shell, right into our hearts. While we might see only plain rock, God can see the sparkling crystals within; God sees the beauty that God created within you, your peers, and the invisible people around you. We as Christians must also look past the rock shell and see everyone as God sees him or her."

Give each person a glass stone. As each person receives a stone, ask him or her to think of one way to commit to loving invisible people. Ask them to put their stones in their pockets and to carry them around each day as a reminder to show God's love to all people.

Do Something More With It

Supplies: DVD player, monitor, the film Invisible Children: Rough Cut,* *film license (described on page 51)*

> Live in harmony with one another. Do not be proud, but be willing to associate with people of low position.
>
> —**Romans 12:16** (NIV)

For an even deeper study of other kids in our world who are invisible, arrange to show the film *Invisible Children*, which deals with the plight of child soldiers in northern Uganda.

Watch the DVD with your youth, and point out how the children who are fighting as soldiers unwillingly become invisible. Discuss the group's reactions to what they saw in the documentary; then compare the children in the movie to the invisible people in your community.

Ask:

➜ Whom do you fail to see or to serve?

➜ How can you become more aware of those around you and what is going on in their lives?

➜ How can you better reach out to those who are invisible?

Brainstorm some ideas.

If funding allows, purchase for each student a bracelet from the Invisible Children store. Challenge the youth to wear these bracelets as reminders to open their eyes to those around them whom they might not otherwise notice.

*Information on purchasing and showing a DVD of the movie is available at www.invisiblechildren.com.

MAKING MR. ROGERS PROUD*

*Inspired by a sermon by Rev. Diane, Senior Pastor in Nashville, Tennessee

Think About It

What does it take to be a good neighbor?

Talk About It

Supplies: Bible; a copy of Cotton Patch Gospel: Luke and Acts, *by Clarence Jordan; optional: an episode of* Mister Rogers' Neighborhood, *DVD player or VHS player and monitor, and film license*

Say: "No other cultural icon in American society who represents being a good neighbor quite like Fred Rogers. Over the years, Mr. Rogers' television show has taught millions of children about being a good neighbor and who their neighbors are. Neighbors are everyone we meet. Geography doesn't restrict our neighbors; neither do borders, fences, nor sides of the railroad track."

(**Option:** Watch an episode of *Mister Rogers' Neighborhood,* and ask the youth, "What message about neighbors does this show send?")

Say: "While Fred Rogers introduced many children to the idea of being someone's neighbor, he was by no means the first person to teach about being a good neighbor. Jesus, for instance, told a famous story about it."

Ask volunteers to read aloud **Luke 10:25-37.**

Summarize the parable of the good Samaritan by saying: "In this story a lawyer asked Jesus to clarify the commandment to love 'your neighbor as yourself' (verse 27). Maybe he was looking for an excuse to exclude someone. He was likely shocked by Jesus' answer. Back then, in Jewish communities, the words *good* and *Samaritan* didn't go together. And to Samaritans, the words *good* and *Jew* didn't go together. In the minds of Jesus' audience, anyone *but* the Samaritan should have been the hero. The Samaritan should have been the enemy, the person to avoid.

"Jesus' point is that even those people we might consider our enemies are our neighbors. And our neighbors are the people he calls us to love, serve, and care for. They include everyone around us—across the street or around the world."

Read aloud a modern interpretation of this Scripture from Clarence Jordan's *Cotton Patch Gospel: Luke and Acts* (available at *koinoniapartners.org*). Jordan sets his version of the story in Georgia during the Civil Rights movement. In his story a Sunday school teacher asks the question; a white man is the one beaten on the side of the road; a preacher and music leader pass by the white man; and a black man is moved to tears to help.

After reading Clarence Jordan's version of the story, ask:

→ What moved the black man to help out? What caused this man to relieve another man's suffering?

→ How can we make a habit of showing love to and care for our neighbors?

Do Something With It

Ask:

→ What would the story of the good Samaritan look like today in our community?

→ Who would the characters be? Who would help whom?

Give the youth ten minutes to work in pairs to write a new version of the story. When they're done, have each pair present its story. Then ask:

→ What challenges to loving our neighbors are in the stories we wrote?

→ How can we stay alert to opportunities to help others?

→ How can we maintain a heart of love that seeks to help, serve, and care for others?

Note that one key to being a good neighbor and being hospitable is to listen and seek to understand others instead of seeking to be understood.

Reflect on It

Read aloud this quotation from Rev. Diane: "We will know we have arrived in the 'hood' of neighborhood when we've made helping others a habit of loving."

Give the youth a minute to reflect on the quotation.

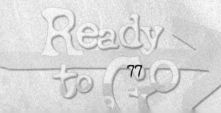

Celebrate It

Supplies: materials for making friendship bracelets (such as yarn, twine, and beads)

Instruct the students to make two friendship bracelets—one to remind them to love their neighbors and one to give to a friend outside the group who could join in their efforts to show love and care for neighbor. You can find instructions for making friendship bracelets at websites such as *www.makingfriends.com/friendship.htm.*

> Do nothing out of selfish ambition or conceit, but in humility regard others as better than yourselves. Let each of you look not to your own interests, but to the interests of others.
>
> **—Philippians 2:3-4**

Part 2: Readying Your Hands

LIVING IN PEACE

Think About It

"If it is possible, so far as it depends on you, live peaceably with all"
(**Romans 12:18**).

Talk About

Read aloud **Matthew 18:21-22**:

> Then Peter came and said to [Jesus], "Lord, if another member of
> the church sins against me, how often should I forgive? As many as
> seven times?" Jesus said to him, "Not seven times, but, I tell you,
> seventy-seven times."

Say: "Jesus teaches us to pray in the Lord's Prayer, 'Forgive us our debts,
as we also have forgiven our debtors' (**Matthew 6:12**). We are forgiven as
we forgive. Because God has forgiven us, we should offer forgiveness
liberally.

"In **Matthew 5:23-24** Jesus tells us,

> 'When you are offering your gift at the altar, if you remember that
> your brother or sister has something against you, leave your gift
> there before the altar and go; first be reconciled to your brother or
> sister, and then come and offer your gift.'

"Again, forgiveness is key to who we are as followers of Christ."

Ask:

➜ How does forgiveness contribute to peace?

➜ What are some other things we can do to "live peaceably with all"?
(Prompt the youth with examples such as keeping anger in check, using
encouraging words, seeking to understand others during conflict instead
of making sure that they understand you first, and listening to others and
asking them questions to clarify what they are saying.)

➜ What are some things that we can do as a group to bring about peace in
our community? (Prompt the youth with examples such as taking a
peer-mediation course and educating the community about stereotypes.)

Say, "Dialogue is the way that leads to peace."

Introduce these steps we can follow whenever a conflict arises with someone:

1. Listen to the person, putting aside prejudices and reserving judgment.

2. Be willing to enter the person's world and experience.

3. Be open to what the person is saying. Recognize that you may change your mind by what you hear.

4. Think about why you believe what you believe and feel the way you feel.

5. Don't use words that cut off or alienate people. If you know you are entering a tough conversation, think ahead of time about what you need to communicate.

6. Reflective listening is sometimes the proper response in heated situations. You might say, "I understand that you said [repeat back to the person what you heard him or her say]"; then the person can clarify anything that you have misheard or misunderstood and feel as though he or she has been heard.

Note: Listening to someone doesn't mean automatically agreeing with that person, but it does mean showing respect and treating that person as a beloved child of God.

Say, "All anyone really wants is to be loved, accepted, and valued."

Do Something With It

Supplies: beach ball, permanent marker

Say: "Listening is difficult, because we think so much faster than we speak. Making our minds keep peace with someone's speech takes practice."

To illustrate the importance of dialogue and active listening, play **Ball Toss.**

Begin by instructing the youth to write several challenging discussion questions (such as, "What would going to college mean for you?" or "What's one thing that every teenager should know?") on the beach ball.

Then gather the youth in a circle and have them gently toss around the first ball. Whoever catches the ball should look at the question on the ball closest to his or her right thumb, read the question aloud, and answer it.

If someone doesn't feel comfortable with the question nearest his or her right thumb, he or she can read aloud and answer the question nearest his or her left thumb. If he or she isn't comfortable with either question, he or she can simply toss the ball to someone else.

Toss around the ball until everyone has had a chance to answer at least one of the questions.

Then ask:

→ When during this game did you find yourself wanting to say something when someone else was expressing his or her opinion?

→ What do you think the purpose of the activity was?

→ Were you able to listen without thinking about what *you* would say if you were the one answering the question?

→ How well do we listen to one another when the topic is something important to us?

→ How can learning to listen and being in dialogue help us cut down on and handle conflicts?

→ What can we do to encourage conflict resolution? How can we be role models for conflict resolution?

Play **Let's Listen,** a game that introduces the importance of active listening.

Have the group divide into pairs. Instruct one person in each pair to talk for two minutes about any subject that he or she chooses; instruct the other youth to listen quietly without interrupting, maintaining eye contact the whole time. After two minutes, the partner must summarize in thirty seconds what the speaker said.

Then have the partners switch roles. This time, the listener should make no eye contact at all with the speaker. Again, have the speaker talk for two minutes, and have the listener spend thirty seconds summarizing what the speaker had said.

Ask those youth who were the speakers during the first round of the game:

→ How well did your partner listen to you? How significant was your partner's eye contact?

Ask those youth who were the speakers during the second round:

→ How well did your partner listen to you? How significant was your partner's lack of eye contact?

Ask everyone:

➜ How do body language and eye contact help let people know that you value what they have to say?

➜ How does listening well enough to be able to repeat back what a person said tell that person that you are listening actively?

Say, "Listening is the first step toward understanding, which is the first step toward living peacefully."

Now play the game **Hot Topics** to help youth practice rules for listening amid conflict.

Break the group into teams of four for this activity. Two people in each team will be in conflict over a seemingly trivial topic such as restaurant choice, best sport, or prom theme. One person will be confront the other about the issue; the other person will listen actively. The other two people in the team will watch the conflict and give feedback at the end. These persons will observe whether the confronter owns up to his or her feelings, expresses why he or she feels a certain way, explains what he or she wants the other person to do to address the issue, and avoids blameful language. These observers also should watch to see whether the listener maintains eye contact, repeats what the confronter said, and replies by saying honestly what he or she is feeling.

Then the listener should take on the role of the confronter and vice versa. This process should continue until the two persons reach a resolution.

Repeat this activity with the observers switching places with the person in conflict. As time permits, repeat this activity yet again, this time with more substantial issues that youth are dealing with.

Note: It may be helpful during this activity to write on a markerboard or large sheet of paper some keys to conflict resolution (such as listening intently, making eye contact, repeating what the other person says, and owning up to one's own feelings). You might also make a small "cheat sheets" that list these pointers. This skill set will likely be new for quite a few of your youth.

Another note: Because we have various personality types, we will all take in information and respond differently. Understanding different personality types helps us understand how to better approach one another. You may want to find a personality test to do with your group and further explore this aspect of dialogue and conflict resolution.

Reflect on It

➜ How hard was it to listen to the others and give them full attention and respect, even if you disagreed?

➜ How did you feel when others really listened to you?

➜ How difficult is it to remember that conflicts are not win-lose scenarios and that we are all on the same side?

Read aloud **Romans 14:17-20** and **Romans 15:7.** These two passages reinforce the importance of treating others respectfully and not allowing our differences to distract us from our shared mission as disciples of Christ.

Celebrate It

Supplies: plain white bandannas; materials for tie-dying (dye, rubber bands, rubber gloves, measuring cups and spoons, empty squirt bottles, and a bucket); fabric paint, permanent markers, or both

Have the youth tie-dye some bandannas and decorate them with words and symbols of peace (using permanent markers or fabric paint). Encourage each person to do two bandannas: one for him- or herself and one to give to someone else.

For instructions on tie-dying, visit *www.pburch.net/dyeing/howtotiedye.shtml* or *www.kinderart.com/textiles/easytiedye.shtml.*

TRULY SEEING OTHERS

Think About It

As you prepare this activity, reflect on this question: Whom do we leave out, sometimes without even noticing that we have left them behind?

Talk About It

Read aloud, or ask a youth to read aloud, **Genesis 1:26-28.**

Say: "If we believe that everyone was made in God's image, then we have to respect people. Respect calls for an attitude of compassion and understanding.

"Each of us has a piece of the truth; no one has the whole truth. We can always learn from one another and, together, grow closer to God."

Read this story from Rev. Diane (or tell a similar story of your own):

> "I had one youth at my church," said Diane, "who was the most delightful young man in the youth group. He was a quadriplegic and could not speak at all. He had the highest attendance in all activities that the youth group did. He was blessed with a caregiver who expanded his parents' care and capabilities of doing things with him. It was his family's commitment that made his involvement possible.
>
> "He was at every retreat, at every class, and made the rounds whenever we did outreach projects. The others in the youth group learned how to communicate with him without words. He was quite bright, but you had to be around him enough to be able to communicate with him. They had their own language. He was one of the greatest assets in the group.... The class wouldn't do anything without him. He was so much a part of who they were."

This story shows someone who might have gone unnoticed if his church had not deliberately incorporated him into their activities.

Ask:

➜ Why might this boy, in another situation, have been left out or left behind?

➜ What other groups of people in our community or society are in danger of being left out or left behind just because they are different?

Say: "By entering this boy's world and letting him into theirs, the youth at Diane's church discovered how loving and caring he was and how much he had to contribute. This story shows how working *with* one another brings about fullness of life and deeper understanding."

Do Something With It

Say: "We need to set aside labels, accept our individuality, and realize that each of us has difficulties and advantages. We do not choose how we came into this world or where, but we do choose how we respond to the world in which we live. How can we further develop an attitude of compassion and acceptance and treat everyone with dignity and respect?"

Have the youth stand side by side in a straight line. Read through a list (germane to your group) of factors related to varying levels of education, family dynamics, economic situations, and so forth that would either give a person an advantage or put that person at a disadvantage. For each item you read, tell the youth to step forward if they think that factor would give someone a cultural or economic advantage and to step backward if they think that factor would put someone at a disadvantage. Ask volunteers to explain why they felt that a certain item would be advantageous or put someone at a disadvantage.

Examples include:

➜ You were born in the United States.

➜ You were born outside the United States.

➜ One of your parents completed college.

➜ No one in your family ever graduated college.

➜ You have been outside your home state.

➜ You have never set foot outside your home state.

➜ English is your second language, and you live in the United States.

➜ You live in the United States, and English is your primary language.

➜ Your home doesn't have a computer with Internet access.

➜ Your home has a computer with Internet access.

➜ Your class at school has never done a field trip to a museum or theater.

➜ Your class at school frequently visits museums and goes to see plays.

Then ask the group whether any other factors should be added to your list.

Say: "This activity illustrates that life is not fair. There are advantages to being exposed to other cultures, the arts, or other parts of the world. There are monetary disadvantages for not continuing one's education. There are advantages to being born in the United States. And there are several other pluses and minuses related to our family backgrounds and the communities we are born into that we have no control over.

"*But* our experiences can strengthen our character and help us overcome the disadvantages that we are born into. And the decisions that we make regarding role models, education, and the opportunities we pursue can create advantages and help make our lives better."

Pass on this pearl of wisdom that Sunday school teacher Betty Ragsdale told her class: "If you can't control the situation, you can control your response."

Then ask:

➔ How might we let differences we can't control such as where we live, our skin color, our abilities, and our disabilities, get in the way of potential friendships?

➔ What factors influence the way we see people?

➔ When has someone shown you compassion? How did you feel?

➔ How can we respond in compassion to the disadvantages that others are facing and seek to understand what they are going through?

➔ How can our life experiences help us develop an attitude of compassion and understanding?

➔ How can you "walk in someone else's shoes" or better understand that person's experiences?

➔ What motto, saying, or word could remind us to be compassionate?

Reflect on It

Ask:

➔ How can we see Christ in each person we meet?

➔ How can we develop an attitude of compassion toward all people? (One answer is to look for what we and others have in common.)

Celebrate It

Supplies: cheap pairs of sunglasses or craft supplies such as construction paper, pipe cleaners, and tape

Hand out sunglasses, or have the youth create eyeglasses out of craft materials. Instruct the youth to decorate these glasses with words or symbols that will remind them to see people through a lens of compassion.

Give each person an opportunity to present what he or she has created.

FAITH SHARING THROUGH RELATIONSHIPS

Think About It

Ask:

→ What words, images, and actions come to mind when you hear the word *evangelism*? What does *evangelism* mean?

Then read the following story from missions and outreach director Mikkee (or tell a similar one of your own):

Evangelism. How many of you shudder at the mention of this word? For many followers of Christ, it is one of the scariest words in Christianity. Whenever I hear the word, I have flashbacks to my junior and senior high school years at my home church. Telling the good news of Christ meant knocking on doors or standing on street corners. This was terrifying! As I grew older, I soothed my guilt by finding an excuse for not sharing my faith with others. I decided that, unlike people such as Billy Graham or my pastor, I just did not have the spiritual gift of evangelism, so I deemed myself exempt.

Then, something happened that radically altered my perceptions of evangelism. During my graduate studies in missions, we learned about sharing our faith. I discovered that evangelism is directly related to living a life of authentic faith. Evangelism is more than stopping people on the street, handing them a tract, and asking them where they'll be spending eternity. Evangelism is more about relationships than words or venue. Suddenly, sharing my faith was something I saw myself doing every day in little ways.

As I have grown in my faith, I have come to realize that I am an evangelist. Each Christian is an evangelist. Every time I walk into the school cafeteria with my friends, I am an evangelist. Every time I help my neighbor, I am an evangelist. I have never had to search someone out to share my faith. The Lord has always brought someone into my life.

For example, after working with someone for two years, I had the opportunity to tell this co-worker why I had a relationship with Christ. I had the chance to say where God had brought me from and how God was changing me. It took two years, but God's timetable is always perfect.

In future friendships, I will realize from the start that I am an evangelist, that God is using me to speak truth. There is no agenda, and my friends are not my projects. I pray that my words and actions will always speak of God's love to the people around me.

Say: "So, the million-dollar question is, How do we share the hope of Christ? Well, we *live*. We live our lives authentically, being with the Lord, learning, growing, and maturing from all that life throws at us. As we interact with others, our lives will speak the gospel for Christ. Think about your friends, neighbors, grocery store attendant, other students, or whomever God has placed in your life. Jesus said to us in **Matthew 5:14:** 'You are the light of the world. A city set on a hill cannot be hidden.' We are called to serve and share hope with the world.

"It is messy business, being an evangelist, because it means wading into the mess of people's lives, as well as exposing our own mess. But seeing a Christian mess up and take his or her sins to the cross is far more powerful than looking good on Sunday. When the people with whom we have relationships see our faith in action, especially during tough times, our faith will rub off on them. The only formula for relational evangelism is 'Keep it real.' "

Talk About It

Ask:

➔ When have you told a friend about your relationship with Christ?

➔ When have friends asked you about your faith simply because of the way you live?

➔ Have you ever told someone how he or she can become a Christian?

➔ What comes to mind when you hear the word *evangelism*? Do you, like Mikkee, get nervous when you hear that word?

➔ Have you ever had an experience like Mikkee where God used you to show God's truth and love to someone with whom you have a relationship? What happened?

→ Mikkee points out that we should not think of others has our "projects" or approach evangelism with an agenda. What do you think he means? Why are these points important?

→ What does your life say about your relationship with God?

→ How is evangelism related to service?

Say: "Service-learning projects give us opportunities to build relationships with our fellow volunteers, with agency workers, with people in the communities we serve, and so on. Take time to get to know the people around you and to build relationships with them. You never know when a simple act of kindness or a small word of encouragement will lead to a life-changing experience of Christ."

Do Something With It

Supplies: paper and pens or pencils

Ask everyone to jot down a list of what they love and value most.

Then ask for a volunteer to stand before the group. Have the other participants jot down one or two things they think the person values and loves by considering what they have seen in that person's actions and words. Then give the volunteer standing before the group between thirty and forty seconds to talk non-stop about what he or she loves and values most.

Repeat this process, giving each youth a chance to stand before the group.

Then ask:

→ How many people mentioned God, Jesus, the Holy Spirit, the Bible, the church, or their faith among the things they love and value most?

→ For whom did we guess that God, Jesus, faith, and so forth was important in his or her life based on his or her actions and words?

→ Whom in our congregation shines brightly for God by their actions? What do these persons do that show their love for God?

→ How can we be more intentional about showing people our faith and values through our actions and words?

→ What service ideas have we come up with that enable us to actively express our faith to the community?

Reflect on It

Go over Mikkee's list of ways to learn more about evangelism:

1. Find out what educational programs related to evangelism your church offers.

2. Spend time praying and reading Scripture every day.

3. Pray specifically for people in your life and for opportunities to share the hope of Christ. Never underestimate the power of prayer.

4. Be honest and open. The most effective testimony involves how Christ has changed your life or what Christ is doing right now in your life.

5. If people want to know more about Christianity, encourage them to read one of the Gospels with you. Always point people to the Bible.

6. Talk to someone who can help or coach you in sharing your faith in inviting ways instead of in "pushy" ways.

Celebrate It

Supplies: a ball of yarn

Make a web to demonstrate how God connects us all through relationships. Have one person hold on to the end of a ball of yarn. Tell that person to name someone who has shared his or her faith with him or her and to toss the ball to another person (while still holding tightly to the end of the yarn). Have the next person hold on to the strand, name a person who has shared his or her faith, and throw the yarn to someone else.

Once everyone has had the chance to name someone, toss the yarn around again. This time have each person, as he or she throws the yarn, name one way he or she can share his or her faith with others or name one person with whom he or she has shared his or her faith in the past.

When the yarn has been passed all around the circle, look at the web you have created. Note that faith holds everyone together and keeps everyone connected. Thank God for the people who shared their faith by example, word, and deed with all the persons in your group. Thank God also for all the people with whom the members of your group will share their faith.

Part 3: Hands in Action

Part 2 included some ideas to jump-start your planning. Now Part 3 will give you service ideas, categorized by the needs they meet, such as homelessness or hunger. The stories in this section come from groups across the country that have done their homework, gotten to know their communities, and crafted projects to make a difference where they live.

Within this section you will find:

- Scriptures for group memorization or discussion;

- stories about young people serving in and with the community;

- project ideas that will help your group brainstorm projects to meet needs in your community;

- guides to help your group pray for the people they are serving;

- sample reflection questions that show how your group's service project can help your youth grow in faith and better understand their community; and

- resources for further learning.

If we haven't hammered it home enough in the first section of this book, let us reiterate again: Involve the youth from the get-go in determining the needs they want to serve in the community. You want to ensure that your youth group is working *with* others in the community, not simply doing something for them.

So, the service project and story ideas in this section are just that—ideas. They are examples to spark your group's creativity and to help your youth generate their own ideas.

Our hope is that you will receive inspiration and encouragement to move to greater depths of community change and not simply replicate projects in this book "as is." Doing so will hinder your ability to turn service into service-learning and to empower your group to address social injustices.

Remember to start with where your group is. (If they're ready for big things, take them on; if they're a new group or have never done service, start small and work from there.) Then work your way toward bigger and more complex projects with youth as co-leaders and hands-on actors in community change.

READY-TO-GO SERVICE PROJECTS

NURTURE CHILDREN

A Call for Hands to Serve

Jesus said, "Let the little children come to me, and do not stop them; for it is to such as these that the kingdom of heaven belongs."

—**Matthew 19:14**

Hands in Action

As a junior in high school, Emmie had a passion for learning foreign languages. Because her mother was a teacher, Emmie had also learned a lot about teaching and child development. She combined her skills and talents to organize a semester of language classes for elementary-age children in a low-income community center. She recruited teen volunteers to join her, and each week they put together creative lessons to teach the children Spanish. They sang songs, played games, danced, and cooked, while learning Spanish. The next year, the teens taught French to the children.

Emmie says, "As an avid foreign-language learner and international traveler myself, I got so much joy out of sharing my knowledge and personal experiences abroad with the children at St. Luke's. It was so rewarding to watch the students get excited about learning French and Spanish. Sharing this passion for foreign languages with the children also helped me build a special relationship with them, and I looked forward each week to our time together." Emmie and the other teen volunteers showed the children that they were important and valued by investing time in building relationships.

"One of my proudest moments," Emmie says, "was when I heard from a parent of one of my students that she had started taking Spanish in the seventh grade at her middle school and that, thanks to her participation in my classes over the past couple of years, she was the top student in the class."

*　　　*　　　*

Amanda's former congregation in Franklin, Tennessee, has worked with an inner-city church in nearby Nashville each summer for several years. The two congregations have grown so close that they feel like siblings—in fact, they are "sister churches."

For one week each summer, the Franklin church teen group would lead a summer camp for five- to twelve-year-olds at the inner-city church and in the surrounding low-income neighborhood. Children would come for community and shelter, not necessarily because they wanted to attend church. Some would come to the church to stay off the streets.

The teens would do everything: cook and serve the lunch, facilitate the games, conduct arts projects, and prepare Bible lessons. One summer, the youth even looked up on the Internet the best way to tie-dye T-shirts and led this craft project for the first time.

The Franklin church youth group did all the planning (with adult coaching and prompting). But once on location, the youth groups from both churches worked together, sharing their skills and talents.

The only leadership the adults did once they were on location was crowd control, and one adult leader played the guitar (but even then the youth told the adult what songs to play).

This once-a-year service experience has extended beyond summer so that when the two youth groups meet at annual conference events, they feel like they are reconnecting with friends.

*   *   *

Josiah went on his first mission trip at age fourteen. He went with a church youth group in his community to Window Rock, Arizona, a small town on the Navajo Reservation. He and the other nineteen volunteers painted houses and helped with a children's program called Kids Club.

Most of the children came from broken homes, even homes where a thirteen-year-old was the only authority figure. The parents often went to a big city such as Albuquerque or Phoenix to find a job, so the oldest sibling would be left in charge for months at a time. When the children came to Kids Club, they'd put aside their tough-guy acts and just have fun playing games. In general, these kids had so many responsibilities that they were not allowed to just hang out and be kids. During Kids Club, they could just be kids.

In response to his experience, Josiah answered the following reflection questions:

→ Why was this program important? *It kept the kids out of trouble by giving them positive activities away from the gangs.*

→ What did you do at Kids Club? *I led three stations: outdoor games; arts and crafts; and Bible theater, songs, and activities.*

→ What ages were the kids who participated? *The program is aimed at ages five to twelve; but all the kids came, because there was nothing else to do.*

→ How many kids participated? *Forty. No adult was left to watch the babies, so everyone came.*

→ How did you make a difference? *The kids saw volunteers who wanted to hang out with them and play with them. This helped them feel valuable.*

→ How did the work affect you and other volunteers? *I learned more about their culture—I didn't know whether to expect tepees. I'm more aware of poverty in America, more thoughtful of people in poverty. Poverty is not just something in Africa—it's something that happens near me. They're just like me; they're just in different circumstances.*

→ Has this experience affected your desire for outreach back home? *The first week back I wanted to do a Kids Club in Nashville. I wanted to play games with kids and love on them. I'd like to do another one in the future.*

Josiah concluded with this reflection:

> At first, I couldn't really see what good I was doing by playing with the kids. But then I read a verse that says: "Just as you did it to one of the least of these who are members of my family, you did it to me" (**Matthew 25:40**). When I thought about that, it made me realize that what I was doing to these kids I was doing to Jesus and that helping these kids and making them happy was something worthwhile. I mean, after all, Jesus died for me; so anything I can do for him is something worth doing.

Project Ideas

→ Prepare an arts-and-crafts project to do with children from a local preschool, Head Start program, or after-school organization. If you are working with a Christian group, you could use the art project to illustrate a Bible story.

→ Organize scrimmages or sports clinics in a low-income neighborhood. Model and teach good sportsmanship and Christian values as you play.

→ Take children on a hiking trip, on a nature scavenger hunt, or to fly kites. Talk about the beauty and majesty of God's creation, and let them simply experience the joys of nature!

→ Make homemade instruments with a preschool or Head Start group; then invite them to sing, dance, and play with you. Play your favorite children's Christian music in the background, or write your own songs.

→ Host a dress-up party at a community center. Talk with the children about how God has uniquely designed each of us and how the Creator loves us as God's children. God thinks that we are all beautiful, and we need to remind one another of that truth.

→ Make sock puppets with children, and use the puppets to re-enact Bible stories for the kids.

→ Simply play. Offer unstructured play time outdoors. Tap into creativity and make-believe, and enjoy the pure pleasure of simple play.

Hands Folded in Prayer

Pray that the children with whom you work would:

→ seek and find a thriving relationship with Christ;

→ be strong in mind, body, and spirit and have all they need in the way of food, love, and daily needs;

→ resist negative peer pressure, in favor of building healthy friendships; and

→ appreciate their uniqueness, stand confidently, and seek to make a positive difference in the world.

Reflection Questions

→ When you were a child, who encouraged you to grow in mind, body, and spirit?

→ How might you tell a child about God's love and salvation?

→ What did you learn about the children we worked with? What did you learn *from* them?

→ What did you learn about yourself from this experience?

→ How did you make a difference today?

→ What might our work here teach us about our relationships with Jesus?

→ What concerns or issues surfaced from your time with the children that you think need to be addressed?

→ What other service opportunities could our group take on to help nurture children?

Find Out More

→ The Search Institute has a list of forty assets (building blocks) that every child needs to succeed in life. Find out how you can build assets into the lives of children at *www.search-institute.org*.

→ Big Brothers Big Sisters, *www.bbbs.org*, supports volunteers as they mentor children in one-on-one relationships.

→ If you're looking for great games to play with the children you serve, check out *Great Group Games: 175 Boredom-Busting, Zero-Prep Team Builders for All Ages,* by Susan Ragsdale and Ann Saylor (Search Institute Press, 2007).

→ Kids Games, *www.gameskidsplay.net*, lists a multitude of games, rhymes, and activities for children.

PROMOTE EDUCATION AND LEARNING

A Call for Hands to Serve

All scripture is inspired by God and is useful for teaching, for reproof, for correction, and for training in righteousness, so that everyone who belongs to God may be proficient, equipped for every good work.

—2 Timothy 3:16-17

Hands in Action

Kate Tanis joined her church youth group for a week-long mission trip with Appalachian Service Project (ASP). She said:

"My role at ASP was to make homes 'warmer, safer, and drier,' a part of our mission that I will always be able to recite. My work crew arrived at the house we were assigned to for the week in Chavies, Kentucky; got out of the van; and observed a state of poverty that we had never seen before.

"There was no running water, a yard full of malnourished pets, and the family who lived in this house had dirty clothes on and did not wear shoes. The adult leaders and youth helpers worked diligently all week in the hot sun, painting, repairing a leaky roof, and rebuilding the front porch so that it was sturdier. There were two young boys, Sam and David, who loved to climb on us, hug us often, and try to distract us from the work we were there to do.

"One day, after our lunch break, I asked the older boy, David (eight years old), if he wanted to read a book together. He retrieved a book from his room; and while I waited for him to read to me, he sat there quietly and waited for me to read to him. It didn't take long for me to realize that he didn't have a clue what any of those words meant or how to read at all—and he was in the second grade. I spent the rest of the week working with him, helping him sound out words. By the week's end, he could read the entire book to me. I'll never forget the look of pride on his face when he closed the book after the last page he'd read to me. What an awesome experience!

"Saying goodbye to David, Sam, their extended family (and all those pets) was difficult; but it felt so good knowing what a difference I had made in such a short time. I taught a little boy to read in less than four days! I've heard that a small group of committed individuals can change the world. How true that is!"

*　　　*　　　*

Sixth graders at a private school in Nashville, Tennessee, mentor younger reading partners, ages five through eight, at an inner-city ministry. The sixth graders aim to develop a supportive relationship with each child while helping him or her with reading skills. They read books to the children (whom they call their "buddies"), help the children learn to read tough words, coach children on their homework, and sometimes just play together.

As a special project, the sixth graders each purchased one of their favorite children's books with literacy grant money a charitable organization. A local bookstore donated canvas book bags. After reading their gift books with their buddies, the sixth graders and the children decorated the bags together as a final activity.

Over the course of a year, the sixth graders become passionate about the relationships they are building with their buddies, and the importance of academic success. The younger children increase their reading skills, which will lead to greater success in school and life.

Here are some reflections from the sixth grade mentors:

→ "The first time I went, I was nervous. Now I'm not as nervous. It is fun. I like that we can help other people. It helps us learn that we don't have to live in our own little bubble and that there are people in the world who need our help."

→ "I have learned a lot from working with kids at the ministry, like how to be patient with younger children and, some of the time, with myself. I have also discovered that some of us are good at being patient and are good teachers, and some are better fit for other things."

→ "If these children do not learn to read by third grade, it will be hard for them when they are older. Our sixth grade class is tutoring the kids by reading with them and making special friendships with them, so that they know that someone cares about them."

→ "This ministry shows me how blessed I am and that God provides and gives his love to all children. This has been a time where I have really grown in my relationship with the Lord, and this ministry shows me that there are many ways to reach out to our brothers and sisters."

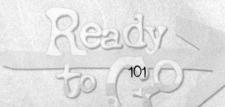

Project Ideas

→ Read to children at a local school. Take your favorite book that teaches Christian character, and talk with the children about their values.

→ Be a study buddy with a peer or a younger student. You can help each other with math, reading, science, or any other school subject.

→ Host a used-book drive, and donate the books to a community center or school. Include a bookmark with your favorite Scripture verse.

→ Start a book club with younger students in an inner-city school. Read a book that's on their level, talk about connections to daily living, then play games that reinforce the book.

→ Lead crazy science experiments or math games at an after-school care center.

→ Set up your own tutoring services for peers at your own school, and help them out. Or start a homework club and invite adults and youth to help out at the church to serve the neighborhood around it.

→ Make alphabet or number placemats or flashcards for a preschool class.

→ Raise money to help build a school in a Third World country. Send to the school's future students some picture cards illustrating God's loving kindness for all people. Pray for those future students to know Christ.

→ Teach computer classes at low-income community centers. Show the students how they can use the computer to search the Bible by using a website such as *www.biblegateway.com.*

→ Collect school supplies such as paper, pens, pencils, and notebooks; distribute them to schools in need.

→ Collect snacks for students in need. Hunger often gets in the way of learning. When students come to school hungry, they start off on the wrong foot. Take hunger out of the picture!

Reflection Questions

→ What concepts, values, and skills are important for children to learn?

→ What has most helped you in your education?

→ What subjects and topics do you most enjoy studying? How can you take what you enjoy and use it to help others? How can you promote an equal education for children in your community and around the world?

Hands Folded in Prayer

Pray that ...

→ local schools would be safe and caring places for students to grow.

→ local schools would challenge students to learn and enjoy learning.

→ Christian teachers would encourage students in their faith through words and small actions.

→ Christian students would find a peer group that strives to live in a Christlike manner.

→ local schools would be free from evil and violence.

Find Out More

→ *Great Group Games: 175 Boredom-Busting, Zero-Prep Team Builders for All Ages,* by Susan Ragsdale and Ann Saylor (Search Institute Press, 2007), has game ideas for both youth and children.

→ Free the Children, *www.freethechildren.org,* gives students a chance to help children around the world through education.

→ *TeenReads.com* offers information on how to start a book club and select books for the group.

→ PBS Zoom, *www.pbskids.org/zoom/activities/sci,* lists fun science experiments for kids.

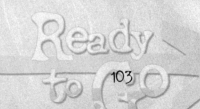

VALUE OLDER ADULTS

A Call for Hands to Serve

Rise in the presence of the aged, show respect for the elderly and revere your God. I am the Lord.

—**Leviticus 19:32** (NIV)

Hands in Action

Julie and her children did a project involving older adults when she served a church in Houston, Texas.

"We wanted to teach our kids the value of serving others and not just receiving," she explained. "So we started doing Trick or Treat So Others Can Eat. We would go to retirement centers to love on senior adults and collect canned goods for others. We trained our group before we went to the retirement center on what to do and not do and let the retirement center know that we were coming and why we were coming.

"Many of the seniors would sit outside their doors, waiting for us to come. If they didn't want us to disturb them, they left the food outside their doors. The kids would put thank-you notes outside their doors. If they were there, our kids would hug on them and spend time with them. We didn't invade their space or homes but just interacted in loving ways where invited. We collected a pile of food for good causes and gave the food to food banks.

"At Halloween, a time when kids are so used to getting for themselves, they're able to do something for someone else: love on seniors and see that they can do for others and have fun doing so.

"We took advantage of other holidays as well. At Christmas our bell choir performed in nursing homes, and we would go Christmas caroling. We'd meet in a recreation room and play the bells for them. The bell choir is an easy way to involve younger children in ministry to others."

*   *   *

One youth group from the West Coast wanted to build relationships between the teens and older adults. The youth started out by offering computer classes in which the teens would teach the seniors. The elders, on the other hand, would help teens with their homework. This exchange was the starting point.

Over time, as relationships developed and grew, the older adults said that they wanted to offer more than just help with homework. They wanted to pass on some of the skills they had developed during their lifetimes: quilting, gardening, and canning. Soon, weekly events and classes were being offered in these subjects; relationships between the youth and their elders deepened.

This project started out as a traditional one and turned into one that tapped into the life history of the adults, covering the lost arts of other times as well as current tech trends.

Computer classes are not the only starting point with older adults. In Tennessee, a group of teens decided that they wanted to do more. They wanted to share their interests and passions. They went on a weekly basis to a local retirement center and offered classes in the arts. These youth led piano, voice, and watercolor classes (things they were learning in school). They too found a satisfying and enjoyable way to interact with another generation.

Elsewhere in the South, a youth group decided to share their love of dance with older adults. They put on an annual Senior Prom for older adults. The night was a mix of old and new, as each group taught the other its favorite dances.

In all three examples, the group took a step toward building positive relationships and using their gifts to meet needs.

Project Ideas

→ Ask a group of senior citizens if your youth and members of their group can be penpals. If the elders have computers, they and the youth could pledge to e-mail each other once a week. (This choice may require your youth to teach the seniors how to use e-mail.)

Topics of conversation could be light-hearted:
• What are your favorite holiday traditions?
• What is a book that have you enjoyed?
• What is one way you enjoy spending spare time?

Or the topics could be more serious:
• How have you seen God's presence in your life?
• When in your life has your faith been challenged?

→ Start a group project involving nursing-home residents, such as scrapbooking or documenting the history of your neighborhood.

→ Have individual youth adopt a homebound "grandfriend." These youth would listen to their grandfriends' stories, rake their friends' leaves, shovel their snow, clean gutters, weed, make minor home repairs, and unload their groceries.

→ Visit a local nursing home for a monthly cards or bingo night.

→ Shower nursing-home residents with love! Take puppies from the local humane society for pet therapy, or invite parents to brighten the residents' day with their babies and children. Perform plays, or sing. (Caroling doesn't have to happen just at Christmas time.)

→ Host an intergenerational tea party where participants bring their favorite tea cup and tell the story behind it.

→ Design and build wheelchair ramps for senior citizens. (You will need to research your state's accessibility regulations, as well as those set forth by the Americans With Disabilities Act.)

→ Make gifts for homebound older adults. Include a card with your favorite quotation or Scripture verse.

→ Write down or type oral histories or faith biographies of older adults. Then consider ways you might use these writings to encourage other people in their faith (such as publishing these stories in your church newsletter).

→ Organize the delivery of meals from the church to members who are sick or hospitalized. If meals aren't needed, ask whether these persons need groceries or medicine picked up.

→ Find out whether the older adults in your congregation, in a retirement community, or in a nursing home have a place to go to celebrate Christmas or other holidays. Consider having youth and their families host these persons. Or prepare and serve a special holiday meal for these persons to show them you care.

→ House check! Are the seniors in your congregation warm enough? cool enough? Are their houses properly equipped? Find out their needs; collect fans, or heaters and blankets. Ensure that their smoke detectors and locks are working properly.

→ Have the youth call and read aloud a daily devotion to someone whose eyesight makes reading difficult. Or simply do daily devotional readings over the phone with someone who is homebound, with both persons reading and reflecting.

→ Check in on older-adult neighbors to make sure that they have essentials: food in the fridge, heat or air for the appropriate season, and medications. The youth can ask whether they need any chores done (such as garbage, dishes, sweeping, or dusting). If food or medications are lacking, you as the adult leader could make contacts with food-service providers or pharmacies.

Reflection Questions

→ What do you most appreciate about older adults?

→ What is something that you might learn from an older adult?

→ What is something that an older adult might learn from you?

→ Why are intergenerational relationships so important?

→ What do you want to be remembered for when you are older? What can you do now to start leaving that legacy?

Hands Folded in Prayer

Pray for older adults in your community:

→ Pray for their safety, health, and joy.

→ Pray that they will continue to invest time and energy in relationships and meaningful activities.

→ Pray that their caregivers will be compassionate and joyful.

→ Pray that they would be confident in God's grace and salvation and not fear aging, death, or dying.

Find Out More

→ Grandparents Day Activity Kit, *www.legacyproject.org/grandparentsdaykit/ introduction.html,* offers a wealth of resources that help youth better understand older generations and suggest creative projects for youth and older adults to do together.

→ Intergenerational Programs & Aging at Penn State, *http://intergenerational. cas.psu.edu,* provides educational programs and practices that strengthen intergenerational relationships and competencies.

➜ Veterans History Project (*www.loc.gov/vets/vets-home.html*, "How to Participate"; *www.pbs.org/thewar/vet_hist_project.htm*) provides tips on how to conduct oral histories with veterans.

➜ StoryCorps, *www.storycorps.net*, says that its mission "is to honor and celebrate one another's lives through listening."

CARE FOR THE ENVIRONMENT

A Call for Hands to Serve

The LORD God took the man and put him in the garden of Eden to till it and keep it.

—Genesis 2:15

Hands in Action

David, a youth worker in Seattle, Washington, named one of of his favorite service projects as director at a youth volunteer program in King County, Washington, "which has teams of youth doing group service projects all over the county in the summertime.

"One group was working with physically challenged youth from a place called the Center. Another group was clearing trails on Squak Mountain. Kids from those two groups got an idea and worked out the logistics with the adult staff so that the physically challenged youth and their volunteers could join the trail workers for a day on Squak Mountain. They had to adapt some of the tools and choose places that were wheelchair and walker accessible; but in the end, all the youth were doing a service-learning project together and clearing the trails. The Parks folks hosted a big barbeque for all the dirty, grimy kids at the end of the day. The distinction between volunteer and client just dissolved through the mutual service. How cool was that?"

*   *   *

A youth group in Canton, Ohio, answered the call to serve by planting trees and getting rid of weeds in a nearby neighborhood. In teams of five or six, the youth went door-to-door in a neighborhood, offering their services to plant trees and remove weeds.

A representative from each team would say, "We're here to do work around the yard—free of charge. What can we do to serve you? We have no agenda. This, for us, is a project to learn how to demonstrate compassion and serve others. We ask only that you let us plant a tree for you wherever you want. You pick the spot, and we'll plant the tree for you there."

> Many local beautification commissions will give free trees to service groups that want to plant them for schools and nonprofit agencies. These organizations can help you make sure that the trees you are planting will be friendly to the neighboring vegetation.

And then the team would proceed with weeding, cutting grass, or whatever the residents asked them to do. Then they would plant trees as their calling card and move on to the next house.

The leader of this group used this experience to teach the youth about leaving a legacy and leaving a place better than you found it. The trees were the legacy that these youth left. They planted, fertilized, and watered the trees; and they would be able to go back and see how the trees would grow over the years.

Project Ideas

→ Build and maintain a community garden; then donate the proceeds to a rescue mission. You might even post on an outdoor bulletin board a devotion about how Jesus is the vine and we are the branches (**John 15:1-11**) or about the fruit of the Spirit (**Galatians 5:22-23**).

→ Place recycling bins around your church. You might decorate the cans with your favorite Scriptures involving the care of creation or artwork that represents Christ. Cans may be turned in for cash, and the money can go to a local park or other environmental nonprofit effort.

→ Challenge your peers to recycle their possessions by giving them to someone in need or another person who can use them. Websites such as *www.craigslist.org* and *www.freecycle.org* can help. If the youth will be collecting items from the public, have several adults present.

→ Host a Don't Drive to Church Day or a Carpool to Church Day, and compile statistics on the benefits of group and alternative transportation.

→ Make puppets with preschool children, and put on a puppet show about taking care of the environment. Socks, zippers, and buttons are great tools for making puppets.

→ Sponsor an acre of rainforest.

→ Beautify the church grounds with a garden of native plants.

→ Design, decorate, and sell organic cotton T-shirts with environmental themes; give the proceeds to a local or regional environmental agency.

→ Plan a "trash art" contest, in which persons create sculptures by using only recycled materials.

→ Do research on endangered species; and raise money to adopt a wolf, bison, or other species of your choice. Visit a site such as *www.defenders.org* for more information. You might also educate yourself on how to develop butterfly gardens, start beehives, or create wildlife food plots to feed native local wildlife.

→ Analyze your congregation's use of energy, and present ways in which members can save energy at home and at church.

→ For holidays, make recycled wrapping paper out of grocery-store paper bags, decorate the paper (using craft paints, sponge shapes, markers, and so on), and either sell the paper or offer a gift-wrapping service at church. Donate the proceeds to an environmental cause.

Reflection Questions

→ How do we honor God by caring for our planet's wildlife and resources?

→ What is costly about living an environmentally friendly lifestyle? How do you decide which inconveniences are worth the time, money, and effort?

→ What personal sacrifices and commitments are you willing to make to care for the environment?

→ What are some ways you can care for the environment in your daily life?

→ How can you encourage others to "reduce, re-use, and recycle"?

Hands Folded in Prayer

Pray that people will . . .

→ change their actions from consuming environmental resources to preserving natural resources.

→ embrace a lifestyle of simplicity instead of always wanting newer and better material possessions.

→ choose to protect and preserve the environment, even if it requires sacrifice.

→ realize their connection to the environment and see nature as a gift, not something to exploit.

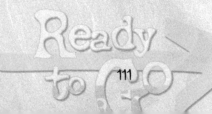

Find Out More

→ Earth Force, *www.earthforce.org,* provides tools for solving environmental problems through active citizenship and environmental stewardship.

→ EduGreen, *www.edugreen.teri.res.in,* is an Indian-based website devoted to educating young people about environmental issues.

→ Global Response Network, *www.globalresponse.org,* promotes global action through international letter campaigns to help people prevent environmental destruction.

→ Kids F.A.C.E. (Kids For a Clean Environment), *www.kidsface.org,* is a national organization that connects, educates, and inspires local kids' environmental service clubs.

→ Save the Earth Now, *www.learningtogive.org/savetheearth,* provides project ideas, activity lessons, and resources that promote environmental stewardship.

→ Nature Conservancy, *www.nature.org,* which works to protect ecologically important lands and waters for people and nature, offers ideas on how to help the environment.

→ Defenders of Wildlife, *www.defenders.org,* offers ideas on how to help protect animals and plants in their natural communities.

→ World Wildlife Fund, *www.worldwildlife.org,* presents ways to speak out for wildlife and preserve natural resources.

EMBRACE PEOPLE WITH CHALLENGES

A Call for Hands to Serve

He said also to the one who had invited him, "When you give a luncheon or a dinner, do not invite your friends or your brothers or your relatives or your rich neighbors, in case they may invite you in return, and you would be repaid. But when you give a banquet, invite the poor, the crippled, the lame, and the blind. And you will be blessed, because they cannot repay you, for you will be repaid at the resurrection of the righteous."

—**Luke 14:12-14**

Embracing people with challenges covers a wide array of hurts in our world. Some of these hurts are obvious: loss of a limb, being confined to a wheelchair, walking with a seeing eye dog, or having to using one's hands to sign and speak. Less obvious are the invisible hurts: emotional scars, suffering from abuse, growing up in an alcoholic home, or addiction to drugs from the womb. People's appearance can reveal other challenges; they dress oddly or wear mismatched clothes, their hair isn't combed, they smell funny, and so on.

These visual and olfactory clues can be symptoms of living on the street, mental illness, poverty, or addiction. All of these challenges show that our world is full of hurting people.

Hands in Action

"There was a young lady from a youth group in Las Vegas, Nevada, who had a brother with mental challenges," Tony, a former service-learning director, recalled.

She had told the group about her family's frustration with trying to get good services and opportunities for him. The group decided they wanted to do something about it.

Over the next several weeks, the group worked to identify organizations that served people with mental, physical, and other challenges. As the youth group talked with individuals at each of the agencies, they discovered that the organizations weren't connected. The agencies didn't know what services other agencies offered or when and how to refer people to these other places.

The youth saw that they had an opportunity to make a substantial improvement to their community. They hosted a meeting and invited all the agencies that they had contacted to meet together so that every organization could find out what others were doing and what services they provided.

From this initial meeting, the community agencies started doing collaborative projects together. The youth for their part decided to offer a four- to six-week program for teens with challenges. The various community organizations helped with this program by providing leadership for each session's topics (which included grocery shopping, setting up a bank account, and recreational activities). And the youth group made a point to develop relationships with the program's participants.

*   *   *

Taylor Bell created TOPS (Total Outreach Program for Soccer), Little Rock's first soccer league for children with special needs, when he was fifteen years old. He found fields, acquired uniforms, put together rosters, and made schedules. Since then, for sixteen weeks a year, he and his teen coaches work with special-needs children on the soccer field. (More than 100 coaches and 100 children have participated in his program.) Now Taylor is expanding the program by training coaches in other states and writing a coaching manual for new groups to follow.

Taylor said, "When you find something you are passionate about, you have to do it. If you don't, then you will spend the rest of your life regretting it."

*   *   *

Maureen is a community hero. She started volunteering with Partners for Youth with Disabilities (PYD) in Boston, Massachusetts, when she was fifteen years old. She said that although persons with disabilities receive service, "they are rarely given the opportunity to give back." Even with her own personal challenges of having cerebral palsy, dyslexia, and other nervous system disorders, Maureen found a way to give back to the community when she started working with PYD. She says that at first her shy nature kept her from speaking up. Now you would never guess that she has struggled with shyness.

To help those challenged by poverty, Maureen started a Pennies for Hunger program, through which she collected $5,000 for her local food bank in the first year. Her philosophy is, "No one is going to miss their pennies," so she asks stores to put collection boxes at their checkout lines and asks friends to donate their spare change.

As a student of physiology and psychology the University of Massachusetts, Maureen has advocated for people with disabilities:

→ She has challenged disabled youth to discover their talents and passions and find ways to make a difference.

→ She has challenged future teachers to make their programs accessible for all students.

→ She has worked as Director of Movement for the Access to Theatre Program, a drama program that is open to youth with and without disabilities.

→ Whenever she has heard people start to complain, she has challenged them to act: to change a circumstance, to challenge a policy, or to make a difference in some small way.

Maureen doesn't consider herself a hero. She says, "I'm just doing what I'm doing. It's just the right thing."

Project Ideas

→ Find books on CD for people with visual impairments. For people who are blind, see whether you can make a CD jacket with Braille writing.

→ Assist Lions Club vision screenings for preschool and kindergarten students. You may also collect old eye glasses for the Lions Club, which will refurbish the glasses and give them to people in need.

→ Help Special Olympics host an athletic event for people with disabilities. Be a referee, a greeter, a cheerleader, or an athlete's buddy.

→ Evaluate your church's accessibility for people with disabilities. Prepare a report or presentation to present to the church leadership; then see what needs to be done and how your group can help.

→ Donate toys to an agency that works with emotionally disturbed children.

→ Collect and donate children's books to terminally ill children in a hospital.

→ Volunteer with an agency that works with the deaf and hearing impaired.

→ Be a special buddy for a child or adult with mental or physical disabilities. Offer to help at school, church, the pool, the library, or wherever an extra hand is needed.

→ Get training to be an assistant caregiver for a child with autism, Down's syndrome, or another life-altering condition.

→ Design and build a wheelchair-accessible community playground.

→ Host a free babysitting night for parents of children with special needs.

→ Collect and donate Teddy bears, or create a box of toys and activity books, for children in an emergency room.

Reflection Questions

→ What can you learn from working with persons with disabilities?

→ In what ways do you—through your words, actions, and body language—respond to persons with physical or mental disabilities?

→ How did Jesus respond to those with special needs? (See, for example, **Luke 5:17-26; John 9:1-12.**)

→ How will you think and behave differently as a result of this experience?

→ How might you encourage others to be more inclusive of persons with disabilities?

Hands Folded in Prayer

Pray that persons with disabilities . . .

→ will be joyful, despite their physical or mental difficulties.

→ will be confident in their bodies.

→ will be surrounded by loving people who can help them function at their maximum capacity.

→ will have the strength, wisdom, patience, and compassion of their friends and families.

Pray also that our culture will embrace persons with disabilities without awkwardness or fear. And pray that the church will be a place where people with disabilities feel welcomed and embraced and where they have opportunities to use their talents and gifts in service to God and others.

READY-TO-GO SERVICE PROJECTS

Find Out More

→ Special Olympics, *www.specialolympics.org,* provides athletic activities for persons with all sorts of disabilities.

→ Best Buddies, *www.bestbuddies.com,* is a national organization that pairs volunteers with buddies who have disabilities, for friendships, jobs, and activities.

→ Disability Social History Project, *www.disabilityhistory.org,* offers an enlightening collection of stories, facts, and history related to disabilities.

Interesting Facts and Figures (From Young Life Capernaum, *www.younglife.org*):

• 610 million people in the world have a disability. If that number of people were a nation, it would be the third largest.

• 18 million people in the world need wheelchairs and don't have them.

• 54 million Americans have a disability.

• This population leads the nation in homelessness and poverty.

• 20 percent of the teen population has a disability.

• Only 10 and 15 percent of churches in the United States have a disability ministry or are planning one.

CARE FOR THE SICK

A Call for Hands to Serve

"The king will say to those at his right hand, 'Come you that are blessed by my Father, inherit the kingdom prepared for you from the foundation of the world; for I was hungry and you gave me food, I was thirsty and you gave me something to drink, I was a stranger and you welcomed me, I was naked and you gave me clothing, I was sick and you took care of me, I was in prison and you visited me.' Then the righteous will answer him, 'Lord, when was it that we saw you hungry and gave you food, or thirsty and gave you something to drink? And when was it that we saw you a stranger and welcomed you, or naked and gave you clothing? And when was it that we saw you sick or in prison and visited you?' And the king will answer them, 'Truly I tell you, just as you did it to one of the least of these who are members of my family, you did it to me.' "

—**Matthew 25:34-40**

Hands in Action

Julie, a pastor, said, "It is part of my job to do hospital visitation. It is difficult at times to involve youth in the visits. In Cincinnati, Ohio, our kids make colorful banners for each person I visit. These banners are computer printouts that say, 'We love you and are praying for you.' The kids put the people's names on them, color them, and sign their names. We do this each week. We pray for each person, and then I take the banners to the hospital with me on my visit.

"One group I worked with made a tape of prayers to share with a person they were close to who was sick. Each person shared his or her own prayers and thoughts. That was a great gift to give someone who was sick—different voices all sharing love and concerns."

*　　　*　　　*

Hannah, age seventeen, went on a mission trip to Haiti with fourteen members of her church in Pennsylvania. Also on the trip were physicians, nurses, and other teenagers who wanted to make a difference in another part of the world.

Hannah worked in a temporary eye clinic, fitting glasses for Haitians who were visually impaired. She learned basic skills in testing vision and the importance of finding appropriate eyewear to enhance vision. She learned

READY-TO-GO SERVICE PROJECTS

how to select eyeglasses for people with various impairments. Hannah recalled that her work was difficult at times, because of the language barrier. "I knew a little French," she said, "so that helped; but we were grateful for our translation book. We would say the words over and over again, to determine the proper prescription strength and fit.

"Some of the patients needed bifocals. The donated bifocals had thick glass, so they didn't look great. Watching the Haitians' reactions, we knew they didn't want to wear them. They had a sense of style, and they didn't want to look foolish. I realized how similar we were—making life decisions based on our images instead of our greater needs. It really humbled me.

"Throughout the week, my goal was to serve people happily and lovingly. We were at a church, so many people knew Christ; but I hope the way I served pointed to Christ for those who didn't already know him.

"I went to the Haitian church service at the end of our trip. The Haitians sang with such ardor and passion. It rekindled my heart and inspired me to love God with that same passion."

Project Ideas

→ Knit hats for people with cancer or for premature babies. Attach a card that expresses empathy and concern.

→ Clean the apartment of someone who has HIV or AIDS.

→ Decorate cards or create an art collage of hope for hospital patients.

→ Help with the American Cancer Society's Relay for Life, and learn what you can do to raise money, as well as educate and advocate for people with cancer. (See *www.relayforlife.org.*)

→ Provide a healthy meal for Ronald McDonald House residents.

→ Create a Caring Quilt together out of paper or fabric to display at a local children's hospital, center for older adults, or hospice.

→ Host a pancake breakfast in conjunction with a blood drive for the American Red Cross.

→ Take calm pets to visit a hospice or home for older adults.

→ Host a community challenge, collecting soda-can tabs to raise money for Ronald McDonald House.

→ Use sheets to make bandages for mission groups overseas.

→ Collect film canisters to use as medicine bottles for hospitals overseas.

→ Learn how to take blood pressure, and offer that service monthly at church to all members (with the supervision of a nurse or other healthcare professional).

→ Promote preventive health. Find out what type of diet prevents cancer, heart attacks, and so forth. Share what you learn by doing a Healthy for Life dinner at the church. Check with local hospitals to see whether they offer healthy cooking classes, and team up with them to educate others.

→ Eating disorders are a disease. Learn about the various disorders, and become a peer counselor to help your friends love their bodies.

Reflection Questions

→ How does our culture usually treat people with chronic or terminal illnesses?

→ How does Jesus want us to respond to people who are sick? (See, for instance, **Mark 1:40-45; 5:25-34.**)

→ What might keep you from reaching out to someone who is sick? (This issue can be scary for teens, and addressing this question can provide some freedom to overcome their fears and insecurities.)

→ What's the best way to talk with someone who is very sick?

→ In what ways might you help care for someone who is sick?

Hands Folded in Prayer

Pray that . . .

→ those who are sick will be healed, or that God will help them gracefully accept their ailments.

→ those who are sick will find comfort—relief from physical pain, support for the emotional challenges related to the sickness, and a spiritual embrace of God that transcends human understanding.

→ physicians will have wisdom to fight disease, courage to treat it, and strength to care for their patients.

READY-TO-GO SERVICE PROJECTS

→ those who care for sick persons will have strength, patience, love, mercy, and compassion.

→ that God's glory will be revealed amid persons' struggles with illness.

Find Out More

→ Stitches from the Heart, *www.stitchesfromtheheart.org*, is a program that accepts hand-knitted hats and blankets from volunteers to give to premature infants.

→ American Cancer Society, *www.cancer.org*, raises funds for cancer research, provides cancer-information services, and runs community programs such as camps for children with the disease.

→ Ronald McDonald House, *www.rmhc.com*, offers housing for parents of children in hospitals, provides family rooms inside hospitals, and brings healthcare to underserved children around the globe.

FEED THE HUNGRY

If one of your countrymen becomes poor and is unable to support himself among you, help him as you would an alien or a temporary resident, so he can continue to live among you.

—**Leviticus 25:35** (NIV)

Hands in Action

The Society of St. Andrew in North Carolina goes to restaurants, grocery stores, and food distributors to get the food that is still good but that, because of store and company policies, will be thrown away. After collecting the food, they give it to organizations that can deliver it to the hungry.

The task our youth group did with St. Andrews was to work with the organization's "potato drop." St. Andrews finds potatoes that were not harvested the first go around. These potatoes are considered not sellable but are perfectly fine. St. Andrews collects thousands of pounds of potatoes, drops them in a field, and gives volunteers some bags and twist ties. Our youth would fill up the three-pound sacks to give away. They simply bag and load the spuds onto the truck; then the potatoes are distributed to organizations and, in some cases, distributed directly to families.

"What I remember about this," one youth minister told me, "is the deeper connection the teens made that the potatoes they were bagging were perfectly good potatoes. Their common frustration was, 'Why are these being thrown away when there are people who are hungry?' Their global thinking kicked in as they thought about the excess of food we're throwing away while people in other parts of the world are starving.

"Four thousand youth worked together on this project, so the teens really felt they were part of something bigger than themselves. They felt like they were really making a difference."

Project Ideas

→ Host a 30-Hour Famine (*www.30hourfamine.org*). Participants go without food for thirty hours and raise money to fight hunger by asking sponsors to pledge by the hour. The project raises awareness and builds community.

→ Prepare or deliver Meals on Wheels (*www.mowaa.org*) to homebound persons or families. Create a placemat or card bearing a message of encouragement to leave with the meal.

→ Serve a hot meal to children at a low-income school or community center. Many cities have Kids Cafes, sponsored by Second Harvest Food Bank, where volunteers can help serve. Visit *www.secondharvest.org.*

→ Cook and serve a meal at a homeless shelter. Visit with the people as they eat. Listen to their stories, and get to know their life experiences. Take time to recognize the value in every person there.

→ Collect and sort food at Second Harvest Food Bank. Say a prayer for the people who will receive the food you sort.

→ Raise money to feed impoverished children in a developing nation.

→ Make shoeboxes of food that church members can keep in their cars and give to homeless persons they encounter. The boxes could include bottled water, snack crackers, individual raisin packs, and information about your church. Or collect restaurant or grocery-store gift certificates to distribute.

→ Organize a weekly snacks drive, and give snacks to an area school where many children don't get enough to eat.

→ Create a vegetable garden. Plant, weed, water, tend, and harvest produce for a local shelter or food bank.

Reflection Questions

→ **Psalm 140:12** says, "I know that the LORD maintains the cause of the needy, and executes justice for the poor" (NRSV). How does God care for those who are hungry?

→ In what ways does our culture stereotype people who are hungry?

→ What do you imagine what it feels like to be hungry or not know where your next meal will come from?

→ How can you be God's "hands and feet" for the hungry people in your community?

Hands Folded in Prayer

Pray for persons who are hungry:

→ Pray that churches, the community, and the government will use resources wisely to help put an end to poverty and hunger.

→ Pray that God will satisfy their physical, spiritual, and emotional hunger.

→ Pray for food banks and missions, that they will have the funds to run their ministries, that faithful volunteers will contribute to their efforts, and that they will be havens of God's love and compassion for the hurting.

Find Out More

→ Feeding Minds Fighting Hunger, *www.feedingminds.org*, provides lesson plans that help students understand hunger and malnutrition.

→ National Student Campaign Against Hunger and Homelessness, *www.studentsagainsthunger.org*, offers a calendar of opportunities for student groups taking action against hunger and homelessness.

→ Heifer International empowers people in impoverished countries to provide for themselves and their families. Learn more about this creative and proactive group at *www.heifer.org*.

→ Second Harvest Food Bank's website, *www.secondharvest.org*, lists of ways to fight hunger in America.

→ Free Rice, *www.freerice.com*, an educational Internet game that increases vocabulary and provides food to those who need it most. For each word that a player correctly defines, the site donates twenty grains of rice to the UN World Food Program.

CARE FOR THE HOMELESS

A Call for Hands to Serve

The issue of homelessness is complex. A common misconception is that every homeless person wants a home; in fact, some do not. What they do want and need is food, a safe place to sleep, and medical care. They also need tangible services: a place to receive mail, a way to do laundry and take a shower, job training, and a place to get food.

> Is not this the fast that I choose:
> to loose the bonds of injustice
> to undo the thongs of the yoke,
> to let the oppressed go free,
> and to break every yoke?
> Is it not to share your bread with the hungry,
> and bring the homeless poor into your house;
> when you see the naked, to cover them,
> and not to hid yourself from your own kin?
>
> —Isaiah 58:6-7

Hands in Action

Picture in your mind a young boy who has been repeatedly abused, along with his mother and siblings, by his father. The boy grows up hating his father and, as a teenager, decides to leave home. He could go to an abuse shelter; but those are run by adults, and he's learned not to trust adults. He could call the police; but the last time his mother contacted the authorities, the boy's father retaliated, leaving her more bruised and battered than ever before. Unaware of any other options, the boy runs away from home to live on the streets.

The sad truth is that many homeless youth today, like this young boy, have run away from abuse or neglect.

The Street Angels Ministry at Missiongathering Christian Church in San Diego supports homeless teenagers. Volunteers gather twice a month to fill backpacks with supplies that teens will need for survival on the streets. They deliver the goods to young people they meet on the streets and show God's love through their actions. Their goal is, "to let teens know that they are loved and cared for despite their situation." For more information, visit *www.missiongathering.com*.

*   *   *

In San Diego, California, another group of young people spent their New Year's Eve quite differently than the way most people ring in the New Year. They were bundled up in a van loaded down with blankets. They drove around the downtown area, not to look for parties but to look for people—homeless people. This group had spent time collecting coats and blankets for the homeless. For this particular evening, they were out on patrol to distribute blankets and well wishes for a healthy year to San Diego's homeless.

Project Ideas

→ Volunteer with Habitat for Humanity (*www.habitat.org*). You could help build a house, make sandwiches for volunteers, teach a class for homeowners, or collect supplies for a family moving into the house.

→ Assemble We Care bags with shampoo, soap, toothbrushes, toothpaste, and favorite Scriptures to give to people at shelters. Or make bags specifically for kids. Include socks, underwear, T-shirts, and other clothing necessities. Consider area-weather-specific needs such as long underwear, jackets, mittens, gloves, hats, and sunscreen.

→ Collect toys and books for children and teens at shelters.

→ Participate in a fundraiser that raises money for an organization that helps homeless people.

→ Start a reading room for kids at a homeless center.

→ Donate clothes and shoes to a facility that assists homeless persons.

→ Collect grocery coupons to give to a shelter.

→ Help maintain shelter play areas for children. Do repairs, and decorate.

Reflection Questions

→ What do you imagine the average day might entail for a homeless person?

→ How might your life be different if you didn't have a home?

→ How have you seen people judge and condemn homeless persons?

→ What are some Christlike ways you might respond to a homeless person in the future?

→ How might you share God's love and hope with a homeless person?

Hands Folded in Prayer

Pray for people who are homeless:

➜ Pray for their safety.

➜ Pray that they will have the shelter and food that they need.

➜ Pray they will have the medical care and attention they need.

➜ Pray that those who work will have the transportation that they need to get to jobs they need to earn money for daily living.

Pray for homeless shelters:

➜ that they will reflect God's mercy and kindness;

➜ that they will provide opportunities for persons to grow in faith;

➜ that homeless persons will feel safe accepted there; and

➜ that the shelters will have the financial resources to provide for the homeless.

Find Out More

➜ National Coalition for the Homeless, *www.nationalhomeless.org*, offers practical ideas for volunteer groups who seek to empower homeless people.

➜ HUD Help the Homeless, *www.hud.gov/kids/hthsplsh.html*, though written for a younger audience, offers practical suggestions for young people wanting to make a difference.

➜ National Student Campaign against Hunger and Homelessness, *www.studentsagainsthunger.org*, offers advice on organizing projects for the homeless.

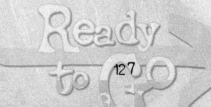

FOSTER HEALTHY RELATIONSHIPS

A Call for Hands to Serve

Lead a quiet and peaceable life in all godliness and dignity. This is right and is acceptable in the sight of God our Savior.

—1 Timothy 2:2b-3

Hands in Action

Natural Helpers® are peer helpers whom other teens naturally approach when they need help. These volunteers are trained to recognize when friends need help and to reach offer them support in their time of need.

Supported by the Michigan State University Extension 4-H Youth Development program, the Natural Helpers® program trains teens to contribute to a safe and supportive school environment. They learn listening and problem-solving skills, so that they can support their peers in healthy decision making. They link other teens to professional helpers when intervention is needed.

One worker with Natural Helpers® said that the program recognizes that "youth are genuinely interested in helping others work through their issues and situations."

The program is making a difference:

➔ One student stated, "I think it is an excellent program because it changes a lot of people's minds from doing something bad to not doing it at all."

➔ A counselor at one of the schools stated that "Natural Helpers® are often involved in making referrals to my office. Also I have a reduction in the minor issues often brought to my attention; the Natural Helpers® are able to help young people deal with those issues."

➔ A worker at the program said, "It encourages youth to reach out to others beyond their own circle of friends if they see someone in need, so no one ever has to feel alone."

For more information, visit *http://web1.msue.msu.edu/cyf/youth/nathelp.html.*

*   *   *

128

"At our church in San Diego, California," Julie recalled, "we started leading family mission trips between Christmas and New Years. The basic idea was for 100 people, from infants to seventy-year-olds, to go to Mexico and lead vacation Bible school (VBS), build classrooms for a school, and offer intergenerational worship services in the evenings.

"It was a great bonding time for families. They worked together on a common goal. The adults went out of their way to include the kids. (It took longer to build a classroom or what have you, but [the adults] took the time to make it happen.)

"The kids learned to see outside themselves and how good they have it, but the adults also learned the same lesson: I have it better than I thought I did.... They could see how families in another country value one another and take care of each other. They saw people who ... didn't take for granted the basic things in life.

"The first year we built houses and led VBS in a dump. The next year we built two classrooms and hosted VBS. All the kids would be on the side playing with kids in the neighborhood; soccer was very popular.

"Our kids also shared their faith with the kids they got to know there in Mexico. There was one boy, Enrique, who was there every day, whom the kids got to know well. The kids would show Enrique their favorite story in the Bible, and he would look it up in his Bible to read it in his language.

"I had been teaching them stories, and they were able to turn around and share their favorite stories with their new friends in Mexico," Julie explained. "They ended up taking my Bible, and every kid circled their favorite verses in the Bible as a gift for Enrique.

"They presented the Bible to Enrique at the end of the trip when we had a ceremony to give the keys to the family we had built a home for."

Project Ideas

→ Host a Bible study or workshop about resolving conflict or healthy communication.

→ Get training to volunteer as a peer mediator.

→ Educate your peers about date rape and how to pursue healthy relationships.

→ Offer childcare during counseling sessions for victims of abuse, or offer parenting classes for single parents.

→ Start a youth hospitality service for your church. Youth can serve as greeters and tour guides for new visitors and can make themselves available to answer any questions that visitors may have about the congregation or neighborhood.

→ Speak at public forums on issues that affect teens or children.

Potential Reflection Questions

→ What are the causes of most arguments and conflicts?

→ How do you usually respond to conflict? In what ways could you communicate better?

→ How might you respond to a friend who is in an unhealthy relationship or who has let you know that he or she is a victim of abuse?

→ How might you respond to peers having a volatile disagreement?

→ What does the Bible say about disagreements, retaliation, and forgiveness?

→ How could you foster healthier relationships with your peers and family? within your church?

→ How can you speak up for issues that affect teens and younger children? What can you do to get your voice heard by the community and by your peers?

Hands Folded in Prayer

Pray for healthy relationships:

→ Pray for children and teens: that they will learn healthy ways to communicate and resolve conflict.

→ Pray that your siblings, friends, and you will make healthy choices in friendships, care for yourselves, and choose wisely how you spend your time.

→ Pray for families: that they will have healthy relationships and ample time together.

→ Pray for the healing of victims of unhealthy relationships.

→ Pray for the church: that it will be a place full of caring relationships.

Find Out More

→ The YWCA, *www.ywca.org*, seeks to eliminate racism and empowers women by providing safe places, building strong female leaders, and advocating for women's rights and civil rights in Congress.

→ Teaching Tolerance, *www.tolerance.org*, provides free educational resources that promote respect and tolerance.

→ Ask a counselor or pastor to speak to your group about healthy versus unhealthy relationships. Prepare questions, such as, "What can we do to build healthy relationships?" and "What can we do to help others get out of unhealthy relationships?"

THE POWER OF ENCOURAGEMENT

A Call for Hands to Serve

Encourage one another daily, as long as it is called Today, so that none of you may be hardened by sin's deceitfulness.

—**Hebrews 3:13** (NIV)

Let not evil talk come out of your mouths, but only what is useful for building up, as there is need, so that your words may give grace to those who hear.

—**Ephesians 4:29** (NRSV)

Hands in Action

Without anyone in the church knowing it, Keith, a youth pastor in Florida, challenged his fifth, sixth, seventh, and eighth graders to a thirty-day project involving the power of words. For thirty days, these young teens and preteens were asked to say only encouraging things to everyone they met—no put-downs, only positive words wherever they were, be it at home, at school, or in the grocery store. These youth were to avoid insults and replace them with kind, loving words.

This project was to be done on the sly. No one was to know what they were up to. It was a secret mission.

Three weeks into the project, the senior pastor called Keith into his office and asked him, "Have you noticed the difference in our church?" (The church had 380 people.)

"What difference would that be?" the youth pastor asked.

The senior pastor replied, "Months ago, everyone was growling about everything. Now, everyone is excited about the ministries we have and the upcoming projects. I am just so grateful that God is doing this."

"Me, too," Keith replied. "Will you come to youth group and share this with them?"

"Why?" the pastor asked.

Keith smiled. "Trust me."

So the pastor came to a youth group meeting and said exactly what he had said in his office earlier. As soon as he was done speaking, a huge roar of laughter erupted from the group of nearly thirty youth. The pastor looked confused. Keith asked one of the sixth graders to tell the pastor what they had been doing for the past four weeks and why. The youth told the pastor about the verse they had studied (which they had all memorized).

The senior pastor's response was profound. He looked at the group (a diverse group of youth in a less-than-affluent part of town) and told them, "Don't ever let anybody ever tell you God can't use you to change other's lives for the better" and quoted **1 Timothy 4:12** ("Let no one despise your youth") to the group.

Project Ideas

→ Hold a card shower for someone who has lost a loved one.

→ Be a Secret Friend No. 1: Pick someone at school, in the neighborhood, or at church to check in with daily or weekly, encourage to do well in school, ask about their day, listen to, and cheer on.

→ Be a Secret Friend No. 2: Have each youth draw the name of someone at church and be that person's secret pal. Th youth will make or send little gifts to their secret pals each month throughout the year then reveal their identity at Christmas with a present.

→ Organize a staff-appreciation week at school or church. Send notes to all the staff, letting them know how much you appreciate their work to help you grow and develop. Include little candies or treats to brighten their day.

→ Collect encouraging thoughts and quotations in a jar. Determine where best to place the jar to encourage others.

→ Encourage everyone at church by sending out birthday cards from the youth group for each person's birthdays.

→ Record or compile a CD of favorite praise hymns that lift the soul. Make it available for the homebound or those recovering from injuries or illnesses.

→ Create and distribute gratitude journals peppered with uplifting quotations and instructing people to record each day five things they're thankful for.

→ Start a member watch. Note who's not in worship, and send cards or notes letting them know that they are missed and loved and that you hope all is well.

→ Create a traveling music group. Don't wait for Christmas. Each month, visit homebound church members and sing two or three hymns. Leave the gift of praise, presence, and food. You might also drop off a CD or gratitude journal you've made. (See the previous page.)

→ Have extra energy? See who's going through physical therapy, and work out with them. Sometimes one's energy and presence goes a long way in helping others overcome pain and encouraging others in getting better.

→ Prepare dinner for a family who has a sick member or has just had a baby.

Reflection Questions

→ When has someone's encouragement bolstered your outlook on life?

→ When have you witnessed the power of encouraging words?

→ Why is speaking encouraging words and acting in encouraging ways so difficult?

→ How can you encourage your family, your peers, and other community members this week?

Hands Folded in Prayer

Pray for encouragement:

→ Pray that God would open your eyes to people who need encouragement, and pray that you would begin to see encouraging others as a priority.

→ Pray that God would give you wisdom to encourage others according to their needs.

→ Pray that God would lift up the downtrodden.

→ Pray that people would see God's love and hope, even in the darkest circumstances.

Find Out More

→ *Conspiracy of Kindness: A Refreshing New Approach to Sharing the Love of Jesus With Others,* by Steve Sjogren (Vine Books, 1993)

→ The Random Acts of Kindness Foundation, *www.actsofkindness.org*

→ Ask a hospital chaplain, school chaplain, or counselor to talk with your group about the power of encouraging others.

→ Host a panel of older adults in your congregation. Ask the panel about the ways others have encouraged them during difficult times.

BUILD SAFER COMMUNITIES

A Call for Hands to Serve

> Your people will rebuild the ancient ruins
>   and will raise up the age-old foundations;
> you will be called Repairer of the Broken Walls,
>   Restorer of Streets with Dwellings.
> —**Isaiah 58:12** (NIV)

Hands in Action

The slogan of Jacobs High School (JHS) Project Ignition in Illinois is "in the blink of an eye—think before you drive." JHS students have adopted safe driving as their service-learning theme. Last year, student leaders planned thirty projects to promote safe driving.

These projects educated students on safe driving skills through holding a Safety Week, accident simulations, student-made signs around campus, and showing a movie about common driving distractions. Their Seatbelt Check increased student seatbelt wearing. One JHS student, Shane, credits Project Ignition for saving his life; after he was in a crash, police officers told him he would not have survived without a seatbelt.

They also created a program called Safety Town to educate children about safety at home and in the community; and they educated parents through a presentation called "How to Crash-Proof Their Kids," and a parent-student handbook with thirty driving lessons.

Project Ignition even re-enacted a prom-night crash to educate students on the dangers of drinking alcohol. The event included a wrecked, smoking car on the football field, a helicopter flying injured passengers to the hospital, and a funeral procession.

The students at JHS are serious about creating a community of safe drivers. You can read more about their story at *www.hdjprojectignition.com*. You can also read more stories from other State Farm Project Ignition grantees at *www.sfprojectignition.com*.

*   *   *

A volunteer group from a church in Tennessee traveled to Northern Ireland as a part of a worldwide peace and reconciliation project. One of their tasks was to restore the flowerbeds outside ten duplex homes and in a ten-unit assisted-living center.

Jacquie, one of the group's adult leaders, said, "It seemed like a small project until the ... organizers told us the significance of the work. We were told that not only did this help restore the tenants' pride and sense of well-being, but it was also a means of protection. It turns out that many thieves see messy landscaping as a signal that the resident was not able to do the upkeep on their home and would be an easy target for crime."

When they finished their gardening, they hosted a cookout in the central courtyard. It took extra time to get the residents' wheelchairs outside; but the residents loved the gathering, as they seldom had opportunities to socialize with one another or leave their homes for such a celebration.

The youth group's other projects included cleaning up a community playground and hosting a communitywide cookout for the neighboring families; the event turned out to be a great intergenerational experience.

*   *   *

In North Carolina, one group of middle-school-aged youth expressed their frustration and concern about the continued presence of broken glass on the sidewalks and paths from their neighborhood to the elementary school, as well as on the grassy play areas along the way. They were concerned that their younger brothers and sisters would get hurt on the glass. As a group, they decided to clean up the sidewalks and the play area and ask adults to help them keep the younger children safe. This group of middle school youth became the catalysts for adults to walk kids to school and to oversee that the playground stayed free of danger.

Project Ideas

→ Work with your local beautification committee to paint over graffiti in a relatively safe area of town. Learn about the cycle of graffiti and the effects it can have on economics, community pride, and violence.

→ Create and distribute a tip sheet to peers and neighbors about community safety.

→ Distribute stickers featuring emergency hotline numbers.

→ Write and perform a skit for children about safety at home and in the community.

→ Host a kids bicycle day with bike lessons, demonstrations, and tips on bicycle safety.

→ Host a neighborhood watermelon party (or popsicle party or ice cream party), so that persons and families in your neighborhood can start to build friendships and support one another.

→ Form a welcoming committee for new neighbors who move into your neighborhood. (Deliver baked goods, give these new neighbors directions for the best route when the roads are wet or icy, let them know where the nearest grocery stores and banks are, give them your contact information for emergencies, and so on.) The more neighbors get to know one another, the more they will support and help protect one another.

→ Form a welcoming committee at school. This committee should be on call to greet new students, show them around, introduce them to others, and eat lunch with them.

→ Campaign for better lighting along poorly lit streets.

→ Create a list of safe after-school opportunities, and let the neighborhood know about safe places for children to be when not at home or in school.

Reflection Questions

→ What makes you feel safe or unsafe in your community?

→ What would make your community feel safer?

→ What people and agencies might you work with to strengthen your community?

→ How would Jesus want you to treat the people in your community?

→ What can you do this month to create a stronger and healthier community?

Hands Folded in Prayer

Pray for safety in your community:

→ Pray for the protection of children, teens, families, single parents, and older adults.

→ Pray that your neighborhood will be a safe place for people to live and grow.

→ Pray that your church will be a safe and welcoming place, free from the violence of our culture.

Find Out More

→ The National Crime Prevention Council, *www.ncpc.org,* educates youth and families on how they can "take a bite out of crime."

→ The Community Safety Series, *www.be-safe.org,* has an assortment of resources for bicycle safety, home safety, alcohol abuse, and Halloween safety.

→ National Organizations for Youth Safety, *www.noys.org,* promotes youth leadership to save lives, prevent injuries, and encourage healthy lifestyles.

COMPASSION FOR VICTIMS OF DOMESTIC AND DATE VIOLENCE

A Call for Hands to Serve

And now faith, hope, and love abide, these three; and the greatest of these is love.

—1 Corinthians 13:13

Hands in Action

Teens Experiencing Abusive Relationships (TEAR) is a group of New Jersey teenagers who want to prevent date violence through education. Through speaking engagements, print materials, and charity events, TEAR teens define violent and unhealthy relationships and tell their peers how to escape those situations. Each of their teen presenters has experienced dating violence personally or has seen how it has affected a friend. These presenters use their experiences to reach others in similar situations.

The teen leaders say, "We hope one day [TEAR will] have an office that would include medical assistance, therapy, group sessions, a national dating violence hotline, and legal help. Our dreams are big, and our efforts to help prevent date violence will never end. Whether it's teaching a class, writing a curriculum for schools, or having a hotline and shelter in the future, TEAR knows that anything is possible." For more information, visit *teensagainstabuse.org*.

*   *   *

Julie involved her youth in work at a local shelter for homeless women and children. "Our service was simple," Julie said. "We would just go there and love on the kids. We would play games and color pictures and just love on them and let them know someone was there."

Project Ideas

→ Paint or decorate a bedroom or playroom for a domestic-violence shelter.

→ Give clothes, shoes, and toys to a domestic-violence shelter.

→ Get training to be a volunteer on a crisis hotline.

→ Host a play day for children in a domestic-violence shelter.

→ Donate household items that make the shelter feel more like a home.

→ Distribute Teddy bears to children who are victims of domestic violence; attach to the bears a phone number that the kids can call for help.

Reflection Questions

→ What does the Bible say about respect and kindness in relationships?

→ How might you help victims of abuse experience God's loving kindness?

Hands Folded in Prayer

Pray for persons involved in domestic violence:

→ Pray for the comfort and healing of victims of domestic violence, and pray that Christ will touch their lives.

→ Pray for the abusers: that they would repent, seek Christ, and live in a healthier way.

→ Pray for the people who intervene in crisis situations: that they would have strength and wisdom.

Find Out More

→ YWCA, *www.ywca.org*, supports policies that protect women from violence and hold perpetrators accountable.

→ Ask a crisis hotline volunteer to speak with your group about her or his mission and ways you could be involved.

→ Ask a counselor to talk with your group about date and domestic violence. Make a list of questions the group wants to explore, such as:

• What is domestic violence? How can we protect ourselves and others from abusive relationships?

• What struggles do abuse victims face, and what services are available to help these persons?

• How can we respond if we know someone who is being abused or we suspect someone might be in an abusive relationship?

Ready
to

SEEK GLOBAL JUSTICE

A Call for Hands to Serve

Treat one another justly. Love your neighbors. Be compassionate with each other. Don't take advantage of widows, orphans, visitors, and the poor. Don't plot and scheme against one another—that's evil.

—**Zechariah 7:9** (*Message*)

Hands in Action

Amanda, a youth minister in Tennessee, told me about one of her favorite nonprofits. The project began when three film-school students went to Africa looking for a story. They had no particular agenda and no preconceived ideas of what they would find or even wanted to find. Once they arrived, they just had conversations with people looking and asked whether anyone had a good story.

They were directed go to northern Uganda where they learned that children were being abducted and used as soldiers in a regional war that had been going on for over twenty years. Soldiers would abduct children, between the ages of five and twelve, from their homes or while they were walking to school or playing in the village.

This led to the three students creating a documentary called *Invisible Children*. The students moved beyond that initial work to launch an Invisible Children organization to educate others about this terrible injustice.

One aspect of Invisible Children is a bracelet campaign. The bracelets are made in Uganda. More than 180 men and women make the bracelets, which are shipped to the U.S. In turn, Invisible Children sells the bracelets along with a DVD featuring a child who has been affected by the war, raising both awareness and funds to effectively make a difference. Invisible Children invests this money into programs such as the Visible Child Scholarship Program, which has given scholarships to more than 600 war-affected students in northern Uganda. The bracelet makers, who have been displaced by the war, are given employment, while hundreds of students can hope for a better education and better life.

Youth groups in the United States and elsewhere can participate by selling the bracelets, sponsoring a presentation at their church or school, or (most importantly) by raising awareness about child soldiers.

For more information, visit *www.invisiblechildren.com*.

* * *

Ingrid, a leader of youth, recalled participating in an event called "Displace Me," a nationwide awareness campaign to bring peace in Uganda. At this event, Invisible Children simulated a refugee camp, prayed for the displaced families in Africa, and challenged Americans to pay attention to the war in Uganda. The participants made their own shelters out of cardboard boxes. They rationed out saltine crackers at certain times to simulate the poverty and lack of food that takes place in refugee camps. They had to make multiple trips to the water station, to simulate water scarcity in the camps. Ingrid remembered, "Even crackers sound good for a meal when you are hungry." She said that the event reminded the participants to be grateful for their freedom and to not complain about trivial matters. They learned about the war in Uganda from a Ugandan speaker. They wrote to elected representatives about ending the war in Uganda. This experience taught the youth about politics, community change, and ways individuals can make an impact.

* * *

During a 150-day period during 2007–2008, youth from across the country raised funds for students in northern Uganda through Invisible Children's Schools for Schools campaign. The money collected was used to refurbish and rebuild ten schools that had been severely affected by the 22-year war in northern Uganda. At the end of the 150 days, more than 1,000 schools across America raised over $1.3 million to begin construction on the schools and residence halls.

* * *

One group of teenagers was particularly moved by the plight of children in Africa. They asked themselves, "What can we do?"

This question led them to investigate what could be done to make children's lives better. Their research revealed a real problem with water cleanliness and dehydration in Africa. They discovered that many people in several African nations have a basic need that many of us take for granted: water.

This discovery led to them founding a new nonprofit organization organized to address this most basic of human needs: water. These teenagers seek to raise awareness of the tragedy that many of our neighbors across the world don't have clean water. The group raises money to build wells in African communities, desiring to offer hope for healthier lives.

Project Ideas

→ Write amnesty letters to free international prisoners of war.

→ Prepare a photo or art exhibit that lifts up stories of human kindness, compassion, or social justice. You might auction off the works and donate the money to an art museum or low-income art school.

→ Research a missionary or Peace Corps volunteer who is doing work in global justice. Ask this person how you could support his or her cause.

→ Raise money to support a global-justice issue.

→ Write a blog post or a letter to the editor of a newspaper to educate people about a global injustice.

→ Collect supplies to aid people through international nonprofit organizations.

→ Educate yourself and others about human trafficking and the signs that someone is a victim of this modern form of slavery.

→ Research environmental crises and their effects on the planet and people's health.

→ Host a Bead for Life party, selling jewelry made by women in poverty in Uganda; send the proceeds back to BeadforLife. See *www.beadforlife.org*.

→ Volunteer at stores such as Ten Thousand Villages, which sell fairly traded merchandise from developing nations.

Reflection Questions

→ What injustices in the world today particularly bother you?

→ Why does Jesus want us to be involved in seeking global justice?

→ If you could solve one world problem, what would it be?

→ "There are no acts of kindness too small." What does this quotation suggest to you?

→ What groups might you work with to make a difference in your interest area?

→ How might you challenge your church or school to make a difference in global issues?

Hands Folded in Prayer

Pray for global injustices:

→ Pray for victims of injustice: that they will seek refuge in God's love, that their faith will flourish, that their needs will be met, that they will find comfort, and that their suffering will soon end.

→ Pray for governments that allow, support, or create injustice: that they will change their ways.

→ Pray for organizations seeking to end injustices: that they will have strength, wisdom, and success; and that they will lean on God's power and strength, not their own.

Find Out More

→ Amnesty International, *www.amnesty.org,* fights for the rights of impoverished people around the world through letter-writing campaigns.

→ Oxfam America promotes programs, emergency relief services, and campaigns to change policies that keep people in poverty. Read about this innovative group at *www.oxfamamerica.org.*

→ International Justice Mission, *www.ijm.org,* is committed to developing hearts and imaginations for justice while teaching the public about human rights abuses.

→ Invisible Children, *www.invisiblechildren.com*

→ Bead for Life, *www.beadforlife.org,* sells beads that Ugandan women have made out of recycled paper. The income generated from bead sales provides food, medicine, school fees, and hope for these women's families.

→ Free the Children, *www.freethechildren.com*

→ World Vision, *www.worldvision.org*

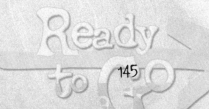

BUILD CULTURAL BRIDGES

A Call for Hands to Serve

Go therefore and make disciples of all nations, baptizing them in the name of the Father and of the Son and of the Holy Spirit, and teaching them to obey everything that I have commanded you. And remember, I am with you always, to the end of the age.

—Matthew 28:19-20

Hands in Action

A group called Youth With a Mission sponsored a picnic, complete with free food and entertainment, to reunite several Sudanese refugees—all boys between the ages of 17 and 25. These boys had lived in the same town in the Sudan but hadn't seen one another since coming to America. They had a great time, eating at an American-style picnic, playing soccer, and learning to play Frisbee®. Volunteers cooked, provided transportation, led games, and just enjoyed time with the Sudanese boys. Three nonprofit agencies, a college, and many volunteers participated.

"Playing soccer is a task-focused activity that helps bridge the gap between language barriers," said Karen Ragsdale, who helped put on the event. "And it enables people to express feelings they can't express verbally."

*   *   *

Youth leader Amanda told of her experience of building cultural bridges when she was in college.

"We went to Baja, California, to lead a vacation Bible school with local children and construct the walls of a new church. [The children] didn't speak English, and we had only one Spanish-speaker in our group. We were at a loss of how to speak or communicate effectively. We were taught one line to say in Spanish, which translated as, 'Come to our house to have fun.'

"We went up and down the streets in a van, inviting the kids to join us; and they just flocked to the house where we were going to do our VBS.

"Once we were all there, our host brought out the soft clay, crayons, scissors, and glue; suddenly we could communicate without using words. We played together and had the best time. After play, our translator interpreted the Bible lesson. It was a life-changing experience—especially realizing that words aren't the only way to communicate."

Project Ideas

→ Build a relationship with a church in another country, so that you can start a penpal relationship either by e-mail or snail mail. One youth group created and exchanged videos of what it's like to be teenagers in their respective countries, including what the other place looked like. Subjects for letters or videos might include:

• What is it like to be a teenager in your country?

• What are your favorite books, movies, and songs?

• What is it like to be a Christian in your country?

• How you are striving to be more like Christ?

→ Teach English to immigrants or refugees. As part of your class, you can read select Bible verses together.

→ Be bilingual buddies. Find a partner who speaks another language and is trying to learn English. Try to learn this person's language. Take turns speaking each other's language for thirty minutes at a time, and correct each other's mistakes. Together you will cross a bridge and teach each other a new skill.

→ Babysit for immigrant families. Do crafts projects that illustrate God's love, or prepare for them your favorite American foods.

→ Make a welcome basket for a refugee family. Include cleaning supplies, toiletries, candles, or a homemade map of your favorite sites around town.

→ Volunteer with a refugee resettlement agency to help teach families how to shop in the grocery store, go to the bank, or perform other daily tasks that we take for granted but might be a struggle for persons new to the country.

→ Volunteer at stores such as Ten Thousand Villages that sell fairly traded merchandise from developing nations.

→ Host a "Visit the World in a Day" event in which you invite people of various cultures to share their food, games, crafts, and interests in a fair-type atmosphere. Consider making the event seasonal. For example, during the Christmas season, have persons from various cultures share favorite Christmas traditions such as carols, games, and foods.

→ Want to go big? Consider an international exchange program with a sister church in another country. Host youth coming to your city or town for a visit; return the favor by going over there.

→ Collect bilingual children's Bible stories, and send them to your sister church in another country.

Reflection Questions

→ What can you learn about yourself, your country, and the world by building relationships with people of other cultures?

→ How did Jesus respond to people of other cultures? (See **Luke 10:25-37** and **John 4:1-42.**)

→ How might you build relationships with people from other cultures in your community?

→ How might you promote tolerance and respect for other cultures among your peers and in your community?

→ How could you build cultural bridges through the Web and other technology?

Hands Folded in Prayer

Pray for understanding among people of various cultures:

→ Pray for respect, understanding, and unity among people in your community of different cultural backgrounds.

→ Pray that schools, businesses, community organizations, and governments might help build cultural bridges.

→ Pray that people would put aside their prejudices and find common ground for building relationships.

→ Pray that your church would be a place where people of all ethnic and economic groups would feel welcome.

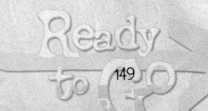

Find Out More

→ Refugee and Immigration Services, *www.risvolunteers.org*

→ Refugees International, *www.refintl.org*

→ World Relief, *www.wr.org*

→ InterFACE Ministries, *www.iface.org*

→ National Conference for Community and Justice, *www.nccj.org*

→ Invite people of different cultures to tell stories about their heritage and experiences.

PROMOTE CIVIC RESPONSIBILITY

A Call for Hands to Serve

Don't just pretend that you love others. Really love them. Hate what is wrong. Stand on the side of the good. Love each other with genuine affection, and take delight in honoring each other.

—Romans 12:9-10 (NLT)

Let us love, not in word or speech, but in truth and action.

—1 John 3:18 (NRSV)

Hands in Action

A challenging decision for anyone is to decide whom to vote for in an election when you know little about the candidates. During an election season, one church had an open bulletin board. Members could anonymously post comments telling whom they were supporting and why—but the reasons had to be based on Christian values, not politics.

This bulletin board allowed everyone in the church to freely learn more about candidates through their faith community instead of figuring out whom to vote for in isolation. Such dialogue can help people make good, knowledgeable decisions and sort through the hype.

In promoting civic responsibility, the question is, How can we teach our youth to espouse what they believe without trouncing the views of others? How can we foster dialogue without bullying? In essence, how do we learn to respect one another's stances and understand differences?

*   *   *

A group of inner-city teenagers signed up for an eight-week financial literacy course offered by a community program in Nashville, Tennessee. First, the youth learned about saving money, balancing a checkbook, and accruing interest. Then, at the end of the course, the teenagers had to open a college savings account; they put a minimum of $10 per month into their account (and they had to show that they had earned it). The agency matched the teens' contributions up to $40 per month; it would would write a check to the college of the young person's choice when the time came for him or her to enroll.

After taking the classes, one young person said, "This is great for us, but my mom needs to know this stuff. My aunt doesn't know this. My sister has a bill collector at her door. What about them? How can this help them?"

The youth did research and were trained to lead the financial literacy classes. that they had taken. These teens offered the classes in churches, school, and community centers—wherever they were welcomed. They taught their families, friends, and neighbors valuable skills in managing money. As time went on, the youth learned about predatory lending practices, such as pawning, rent-to-own, car-title lending, and payday lending (where people borrow money at a high interest rate against future paychecks). Such forces work against low-income workers and often keep them trapped in a cycle of dependence. "How can businesses do this to us? How can they get away with this?" asked one of the youth in the program. The teens did some research to better understand what was happening and how predatory lenders got away with taking advantage of people.

The youth contacted business leaders, lawyers, and others in the community who could help the teens understand predatory lending. As of this writing, these young people are exploring how to change laws to regulate predatory loans and right this injustice in low-income neighborhoods.

Anderson, an adult who has worked tirelessly with these youth, said, "Our kids received financial education and said, 'Yeah, but.' [They had an] interest in . . . having a bigger impact . . . and being more connected [to the victims of predatory lending]."

Anderson explained how this effort moved through the crawl, walk, and run stages:

> "We began to crawl when we moved out of purely adult-led workshops to teens starting to take on roles in leading financial education sections of our workshops.

> "We began to walk at the point when youth started asking, 'What about my family?' [These questions] led the youth to research these issues that were specific to their neighborhoods. They turned their research into workshops to educate the community.

> "Then we started our run phase when youth asked, 'How can we implement our policy?' Our youth are building a broader coalition of interested community folks to look at policy and loopholes in policy that allows businesses to prey on low-income communities."

READY-TO-GO SERVICE PROJECTS

Anderson said that this transition from crawl to walk to run took place over five years. "Development over time is key," he remarked. "The growth came by baby steps. We didn't start thinking we would address piracy issues. We did one project then, in reflection, thought about how we could go deeper."

Project Ideas

→ Publicize elections and voting.

→ Propose a congressional bill or voice a legislative concern to your legislator.

→ Start a petition to right an injustice or support a letter-writing campaign for a cause you're passionate about.

→ Get involved with your local YMCA Youth and Government program. This program teaches teens to recognize community problems and lobby government officials.

→ Write an article for your church newsletter about the importance of being an involved citizen.

→ Host a mock voting booth for children and youth. Tally the results and announce them on a website or in a neighborhood newspaper.

→ Host a forum about an important issue to learn more and educate others.

→ Learn more about human-rights violations worldwide and what your group can do to fight these injustices.

→ Become an advocate! Find a cause, learn about it, and educate others. Stick with it. Host a presentation on this cause at your church, and offer follow-up opportunities so that church members can get involved in addressing this issue.

Reflection Questions

→ Why is civic responsibility important?

→ Why is it important for people of faith to be involved in voting and to pay attention to local and national politics?

→ How should a Christian respond to bills and laws that are contrary to what she or he believes to be right and true?

→ What inspires *you* to take a stand on a particular issue?

→ What happens if people don't speak up or act for what they believe is right?

→ How can you encourage your community's leaders to make decisions for the well-being of everyone in the community?

→ Why is praying for our community leaders important? What difference can it make?

→ Which community, state, national, and world leaders can you commit to praying for this week?

Hands Folded in Prayer

Pray that:

→ Christian leaders on local, state, national, and international levels will live godly lives of strong conviction and make wise decisions.

→ Christian citizens will live honorable lives, using their gifts and talents to strengthen their communities.

→ individuals will find ways to actively address injustices in their communities.

→ new Christian leaders would take a stand on behalf of Christian principles.

→ the church would take an active role in strengthening our communities.

Find Out More

→ Youth Noise, *www.youthnoise.com*

→ YMCA Youth and Government, *www.ymcayg.org*

→ Citizenship Washington Focus, *www.4hcwf.org*

→ The Center for Public Justice, *www.cpjustice.org*

→ Invite a Christian politician to speak with your youth group. Ask him or her what being a Christian in the world of politics is like and how the youth in your group can make a difference on issues that are important to them.

SUPPORT FAMILIES

Family here includes orphans, widows, foster-care children, single-parent families, and other families that have struggled to find a steady support system.

A Call for Hands to Serve

Religion that is pure and undefiled before God, the Father, is this: to care for orphans and widows in their distress, and to keep oneself unstained by the world.

—**James 1:27**

Hands in Action

Amanda recalls a project she was involved with in Black Mountain, North Carolina. She has sent ten groups of teens to the Presbyterian Home for Children to do essential repairs and yard work.

The amazing thing about these simple tasks is that the youth groups would come back amazed that orphans in today's world still existed. The youth were deeply concerned about the challenges the children face in the school systems; the other students treated them as outcasts. The youth groups would come back with more understanding and compassion for those who do not have a "regular" home.

*   *   *

In 1995, when Aubyn Burnside was ten years old she learned that the average foster child moves three to four times during his or her youth. Aubyn further saddened to realize that the children didn't have suitcases and usually moved their belongings in garbage bags. Wanting to give these children more dignity and a way to protect their treasures, Aubyn and her brother, Welland, founded Suitcases for Kids. They invited churches and youth organizations to help collect suitcases for every foster child in their county. The enthusiasm spread from county to county and eventually across the United States.

Twelve years later, the Burnsides are still involved—primarily handling logistics and speaking around the country. They have collected, cleaned, and delivered over 25,000 suitcases. They estimate that volunteers in 47 countries have donated hundreds of thousands of suitcases, backpacks, and duffel bags. They are excited about the suitcases, but they are even more thrilled about the increased awareness of the needs of children in foster care. The Burnsides that believe that one person can make a difference, and they challenge others to make a difference with the passions and skills God has given them. For more information, visit *www.suitcasesforkids.org.*

Project Ideas

→ Help a widow or a single mother with yard work and home repairs.

→ Partner up with adults who have automechanical skills, and offer a free monthly oil-change service at church for widows and single mothers.

→ Babysit (for free) for single mothers.

→ Befriend a child from a single-parent or foster home. Offer to help with homework, play sports together, cook dinner together, or share a hobby.

→ Partner with an orphanage to provide prayer and supplies.

→ Donate frequent-flier miles to families seeking to adopt international orphans.

→ Plan a fundraiser to collect funds for a Christian orphanage.

→ Use the holidays as an excuse to reach out in love to single parents, widows, widowers, and others in your church. Holidays can be difficult if someone has lost a loved one or if money is tight. Collect and distribute Thanksgiving baskets for Thanksgiving (canned goods, turkey, and so forth). Make and give fudge at Valentine's Day. Find out what needs they have, and be Santa's helpers at Christmas to ensure that their holidays are bright and merry! Use your imagination.

→ Host a seminar about foster care; ask families in your congregation to discern whether God is calling them to be a foster family.

→ Put together backpacks full of school supplies, toiletries, or both for children in foster care.

Reflection Questions

→ How does the Bible tell us to care for widows and orphans? (See, for example, **Exodus 22:22; 1 Timothy 5:3-8;** and **James 1:27**.) If the Bible were being written today, what other groups of people might Scripture tell us to care for?

→ Why, do you think, does the Bible tells us to care for widows and orphans, as well as other hurting families?

→ What might make life more difficult for widows and widowers, and how might you care for them?

→ What would it feel like to be an orphan, and how might you love an orphan?

→ What issues do you imagine that foster children struggle with, and how could you help these children with these struggles?

→ What are some of the unique issues that you've seen single-parent families struggle to overcome? How might you help to ease their load?

Hands Folded in Prayer

Pray for vulnerable families in your community:

→ Pray for their safety and health.

→ Pray for them to know Christ and be surrounded by Christian friends.

→ Pray that God would be near them through all of life's challenges and that they may know God's presence and care.

→ Pray for the caregivers of children: that they may find God's strength, wisdom, patience, and love.

→ Pray for orphanages: for safety, health, loving caregivers, and funding to do their work effectively.

→ Pray for single parents: for wisdom, grace, and strength.

→ Pray for widows: for comfort, loving support, and healing.

→ Pray for foster children and children in single-parent homes: for them to to know that they are loved and valued and for them to live an abundant life.

→ Pray that loving people and churches would embrace vulnerable families.

Find Out More

→ Catholic Charities USA, *www.catholiccharitiesusa.org*

→ FamilyLife Today, *www.familylifetoday.org*

→ Ask a family counselor to talk with your group about qualities of healthy families.

→ Invite a panel of people involved with foster care and adoption to educate your group on the specific needs of foster children, orphans, foster families, and adoptive families.

→ *Aging Out* is a 2005 PBS documentary about teens who are "aging out" of foster care. Visit *www.pbs.org/wnet/agingout/index-hi.html* for more information.

Ready to Go

REMEMBER THE PRISONERS

A Call for Hands to Serve

Remember those are in prison, as though you were in prison with them; those who are being tortured, as though you yourselves were being tortured.

—Hebrews 13:3

Hands in Action

This area of service raises red flags for many people. We would never recommend that you put your youth group in a dangerous situation. But we would be amiss if we did not recognize that prisons and prisoners are a part of our community.

How can we offer grace to prisoners? How can we better understand the underlying reasons so many people are in prison? How did they get there? What can we do to prevent other youth from becoming part of this system? What alternatives can we offer for those in prison who are mentally ill? What changes could make the criminal justice system more fair?

When Jacob Komar from Connecticut found thirty outdated computers being discarded from a school, he (then nine years old) decided to find a home for them. He started Computers for Communities, Inc., an organization that works with volunteers in prisons and schools to refurbish and distribute computers to people who can't afford them. Through distributing over one thousand computers, they have empowered many volunteers and helped recipients develop job skills. Prisoners with no former computer training now have marketable job skills in a technology-based workplace. For more information, visit *www.computers4communities.org.*

*   *   *

The Urban Passage, Inc. serves youth held in custody at the Northern Virginia Juvenile Detention Home. The organization partners with community volunteers to teach, inspire, and mentor youth in custody. Urban Passage's goal is to be a partner with the detained youth in rebuilding their lives, getting access to educational and social support, economic counseling, and spiritual mentoring. The Urban Passage wants to see youth move from the life they have always known to the life that God intended for them.

Since 2005, The Urban Passage has partnered with Glories Happy Hats to sew hats for terminally ill children in a local hospital. The detention-center youth are responsible for the design, production, and quality assurance of the hats. Volunteers work alongside them, encouraging the youth to persevere when they are overwhelmed by the task or discouraged by setbacks.

When the hats are completed, the youth deliver the hats to families in the hospitals. The children get to choose a hat and, if they wish, a hat for a friend or sibling.

The Urban Passage President Kimberly Moore said, "I love this program because young people get an opportunity to contribute to the happiness of others. The teens' lives are difficult, but when they meet the sick children, they begin to realize that they have a lot to be grateful for." The program makes a lasting impact on the teens because they realize that they have a positive contribution to make to society, and the community values their efforts. The teens love it too. After they are released from the detention program, they often ask to come back to be a part of the Happy Hats program.

Find out more at *www.theurbanpassage.org* or *www.glorieshappyhats.org*.

Project Ideas

→ Cook a meal, and eat with former prisoners in a halfway house.

→ Make welcome boxes for residents at a transitional living center. Include items such as a Bible, bookmark, gum, a list of free community activities, and a card with information about your congregation.

→ Adopt a family in which a parent is in prison. Invite the family to a picnic in the park and to special church events, send them cards throughout the year, and attend school events together.

→ Start a library for prisoners. Collect and send them inspirational and educational books. Provide opportunities for them to discuss what they've learned about faith, love, and so forth by reading. If you are starting a library for a juvenile-detention facility, you might work from a list of your youth group's favorite books.

→ Send holiday cards or care packages to prisoners for special occasions.

→ Start a Bible study in a juvenile-detention facility.

> Sometimes persons in prisons and halfway houses have stipulations on their sentences or paroles that prohibit them for having contact with minors. Call your local agency to find out about legalities that might affect your service projects.

Reflection Questions

→ How does the Bible command us to respond to prisoners? (See, for example, **Isaiah 61:1; Matthew 25:34-40; Hebrews 13:3.**)

→ What do you think would being in prison or having a family member in prison would feel like? What special needs might a prisoner have?

→ How might you show God's love and mercy to a prisoner, a former prisoner, or a prisoner's family?

→ How will your new understanding of prisoners affect the way you respond to prisoners in the future?

Hands Folded in Prayer

Pray that individuals in prison might have:

→ repentant hearts;

→ well-being, health, and safety;

→ a love for Christ and godly things;

→ Christian friends; and

→ grace in their transition to life outside prison and that they might find a job and a place to live and be restored to their families and communities.

Pray for prisons:

→ Pray for safety within the prisons.

→ Pray that persons who work in prisons will treat prisoners with love and dignity.

Pray that our community can become increasingly more like God's kingdom so that one day, prisons will no longer be necessary.

Find Out More

→ Prison Fellowship, *www.prisonfellowship.org*

→ Angel Tree, *www.angeltree.org*

→ Invite a former prisoner to give his or her testimony to your youth group.

→ Visit a prison, and talk with some of the inmates.

READY-TO-GO SERVICE PROJECTS

Part 4: Putting the Pieces Together

So far in this book, you've learned about service-learning; heard stories from others; and gathered tips, ideas, and resources that will help your youth launch their own service-learning projects. As you undertake this journey of becoming servant leaders, the hope is that you and your youth will learn more about your community and reflect God's compassion and love to a dark and hurting world.

You can expect that as your youth identify their gifts and passions, they will discover new ways to positively influence the community.

What Else Do You Need to Know About Tackling Issues and Projects?

Don't get stuck planning grandiose projects. Just find a way to make a difference soon. What can you do this month? What can you do this week? What small thing can you do today?

Don't be satisfied with one-time projects, either. Little projects are a great way to get started, but making a lasting impact requires a long-term investment. If you can, join hands with another group to double the investment and impact. Follow where God opens doors and guides you.

First Projects: A Little More on the Subject

In Part 3 of this book, examples were given of small (crawl), medium (walk), and large (run) service-learning projects. For groups that are new to service-learning, take things slow and pace yourselves. Seek out projects that you can complete in a short period of time with limited resources. Choose projects that will give your youth a sense of accomplishment but that will make them eager to go deeper. Examples include the Angel Tree project, sorting goods at a food bank, or reading with younger children.

As the youth become eager to do more, you will be able to spot potential leaders for your next project. With each new project, you can hand over more leadership responsibility to the youth until they are in charge and you are simply serving as an adviser.

To make a sustained, long-term commitment to service-learning, keep your group's energy flowing and its numbers growing. To do so, be aware that youth get involved with service for various reasons:

→ Some are task-oriented. They like to have clear, concrete tasks to complete. These youth are most invested in the service-learning experience and in relationships with others in the group when they have something to do.

→ Others like to think and study. They think through issues and get involved with issues that are important to them.

→ Still other youth are naturally relationship oriented. They want to be involved in doing good things for other people and are "wired" for service.

→ Some youth just want to have fun—and they can add a spark of joy to even the most mundane projects.

Keep these variants in mind, and use them to your advantage as you incorporate service-learning into your ministry.

Getting the Word Out

Enthusiasm toward a service-learning project will wane if no one shows up for planning meetings or if, once the project has been planned, no one shows up to do the actual work. Those in leadership roles—whether youth or adults—need to work hard to get the word out about meetings and the project itself. A successful service-learning program requires a strong communication strategy.

So, identify your teens' preferred communication methods by taking an informal survey. Knowing how best to reach your youth will save you a lot of headaches. A sample survey can be found on page 175. Means of communication can include:

- phone calls
- text messaging
- church website
- announcements during worship
- church bulletin
- e-mail
- church newsletter
- social networking website
- fliers
- personal invitations

For each project you do, encourage your youth to identify five people whom they will contact and tell about the service opportunity. These people could be youth in your group who are no longer active or friends and peers outside your group.

Celebrating

Celebrations show appreciation, keep the group energized, and bolster the youths' self-esteem. Your celebration should be unique to your group, so determine how your group likes to celebrate and be recognized. You'll get ideas for acknowledging individual efforts and making the event fun and meaningful. Keep a record of what each youth in your group likes as special

"I grew up with one of those 'mean' mothers who didn't let her kids watch cartoons on Saturday mornings. . . . Instead, she took me and my brother Mark to a food pantry every week. She was an intake coordinator, who would meet with clients who needed food for their families once a month. My brother and I were stockers and baggers back in the pantry. We goofed off and made little games out of stocking the mac-and-cheese and peanut butter on the shelves. Although I complained about getting up early and missing those cartoons, I didn't mind this weekend ritual a bit. And I think it's because this act of service was actually *fun* to me. It was hard for me to believe and explain to my friends that I thought this kind of volunteer work was fun. Those Saturdays of service proved to be a lasting lesson for me: that service not only makes you feel good but you can always make it fun to serve too!"

—Kate Tanis

treats. You could refer to this list when celebrating birthdays and special events.

A sample celebration and recognition survey can be found on page 176.

Motivating

What motivates your youth will vary according to personality and interests. Some youth may achieve satisfaction from simply making a difference; some may be motivated by the opportunity to use their gifts and skills; others look forward to being part of a group or being recognized by their peers; others may feel that they are expected to participate in service. Still, others will be motivated by practical concerns, such as having service experience to list on a college, scholarship, or National Honor Society application.

The hope is that over time and with guidance from you and other adult leaders, youth who are motivated by recognition or personal gain will become increasingly motivated by compassion and God's call to serve others.

For a survey you can use to identify the current motivations of your youth, see page 177.

Think Safety Always, First, and Foremost

Check your congregation or denomination's policies on transportation, permission and release forms, youth-adult ratios, and other matters involving safety and security. Keep these things in mind:

➜ Have on hand fully stocked first-aid kits, extra cash, water, seasonal supplies (such as sunscreen or blankets), and mobile phones programmed with emergency contact numbers. Have a Plan B ready if things go amiss.

READY-TO-GO SERVICE PROJECTS

→ Train your adult volunteers and chaperones. Prepare them to participate in the service activities, inform them of pertinent rules and policies, and let them know what to expect at the site where you'll be working.

→ Orient where you need to orient. Let all the people involved in your service project know the itinerary, what work will be involved, and so on.

If you are working with an outside agency, you'll need to know their safety rules and regulations as well. For instance, these organizations may have a policy about taking photos; you may need the agency's permission to post pictures of an agency-sponsored service project on your church website. Know these policies, and respond accordingly.

Doing the homework on the front end can save you a lot of headaches. The goal should be to keep youth safe while they're hard at work doing good things for the sake of God's kingdom.

Closing Thoughts

Use your group's gifts, talents, and passions. Give money to causes that your youth deem important. Encourage them to speak loudly about their cause, to love people wildly, to pray for people diligently, and to praise and thank God for the changes they see taking place, step by step, little by little. Encourage your youth to be patient, because lasting change takes time.

Remind the youth never to let anyone look down on them because they are young. (See **1 Timothy 4:12.**) Rather, they should use their youthful energy and idealism to their advantage. This is their time.

> Youth worker Jacquie offers these tips:
>
> "First, invite your group to start praying for the project several weeks before the actual project begins. This sets the tone for service in wonderful ways.
>
> "Then be clear about your behavioral and team expectations, but also challenge the youth to throw out any expectations they have. . . . Challenge them to be open to any and all ways God will be at work, not just the tasks that they want or have dreamed about. (This includes getting lost, flat tires, and unorganized worksites.) Remember that when these things happen, you set the tone for the response! Prepare yourself for how you will react when (not if) these issues happen."

Service Service Service Service

READY-TO-GO SERVICE PROJECTS

Reproducible Pages

SERVANT LEADERSHIP TRIANGLE

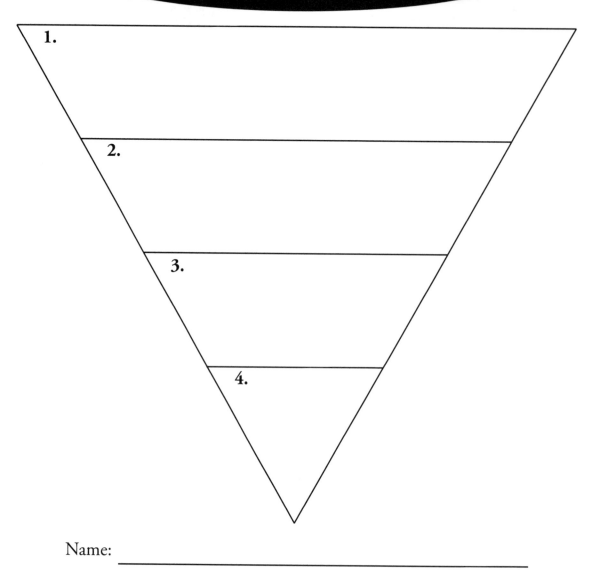

1.

2.

3.

4.

Name: _____

- In level 1, write qualities of a good servant leader.
- In level 2, write ways you've served in your home, school, church, and community.
- In level 3, write leadership roles that you've had.
- In level 4, write three skills you could use as a servant leader.

SERVICE-LEARNING CONTINUUM

Rank each item in order from service to service-learning. Place the item that represents the highest level of service-learning at the top and the item that most represents service without learning at the bottom. Rank the other eight items accordingly.

Service-learning

_____ → Tutoring a student who is struggling in math

_____ → Sponsoring an exchange student from another country

_____ → Reading the newspaper

_____ → Making a peanut-butter-and-jelly sandwich for your little sister

_____ → Giving blood

_____ → Building houses for families in need during spring break

_____ → Visiting a resident of a nursing home

_____ → Talking to others about service

_____ → Serving dinner to the homeless

_____ → Organizing a group to protest a decision to locate a landfill near a residential area

_____ → Teaching financial-literacy courses for persons who don't know how to manage their money

Service

A MONTH OF KINDNESS

Consider setting aside an entire month as Kindness Month, a time to spread kindness through little things you do every day that show Christ's love and light to others. Below are some ideas you might consider for Kindness Month. Add your own ideas so that you have one idea for each day.

1. Be kind to someone who isn't expecting it.

2. Memorize a Bible verse about kindness, and recite it for others.

3. Take time to listen to a friend who needs to talk.

4. Cook or buy dinner or dessert for a friend.

5. Walk a dog for (or with) an elderly neighbor.

6. Encourage someone through your words and actions.

7. Help a peer with a school subject he or she struggles with.

8. Memorize a verse about God's unconditional love, and write this verse in a card that you give to a friend.

9. Help someone carry books or groceries.

10. Brainstorm kind things that you can do in your school or home.

11. Pick up trash around the neighborhood.

12. End a feud or grudge by being the first to say, "I'm sorry."

13. Read a New Testament story about Jesus' kindness to a child.

14. Babysit for free for parents who need a break.

15. Send a thank-you note to someone special who isn't expecting it.

16. Thank friends or family for something they've done for you.

17. Volunteer to take on extra tasks at church (in the nursery, with the offering, and so on).

18. Teach a young child something new.

19. Shovel snow or rake leaves for an elderly neighbor.

20. Memorize a verse about helping the poor, and find a way to put it into practice.

21. Write a letter to someone who needs an encouraging word.

22. Bake cookies for a friend.

23. Read a book to a child.

24. Go the whole day without complaining or saying mean things to or about others.

A LOOK AT YOU

1. Circle the traits that you think describe you.

2. Identify the three traits that you think people most often associate with you.

3. Identify the three traits that you would like to strengthen or make more a part of who you are.

ACTIVE	FAIR	MATURE
ADAPTABLE	FRIENDLY	NEAT
ADVENTURESOME	FUNNY	OPEN MINDED
AMBITIOUS	GENTLE	ORGANIZED
APPRECIATIVE	GIVING	PATIENT
BOLD	HARD WORKING	PLAYFUL
BRAVE	HELPFUL	PRACTICAL
CALM	HONEST	QUICK WITTED
CARING	HOSPITABLE	RESOURCEFUL
CHEERFUL	HUMBLE	RESPECTFUL
CLEVER	IMAGINATIVE	RESPONSIBLE
CONFIDENT	IMPROVING	STRONG
COURAGEOUS	INFLUENTIAL	SUPPORTIVE
CREATIVE	INSIGHTFUL	THOROUGH
CURIOUS	JOYFUL	TRUSTWORTHY
DETERMINED	KIND	UNDERSTANDING
ENERGETIC	LOVING	VIVACIOUS
ENTHUSIASTIC	LOYAL	WISE

YOU AT YOUR BEST

What are *you* good at? What do *you* enjoy doing? What do people ask you for help with? Circle the words that best describe your gifts, talents, and passions.

ACTING	ENCOURAGING	PUBLICIZING
BLOGGING	FIXING THINGS	READING
BUILDING	HOSTING	SELLING
CARING	INFLUENCING	SEWING
COLLECTING	LISTENING	SINGING
COMPUTER PROGRAMMING	MAKING DECISIONS	SONG WRITING
COOKING	MEMORIZING	STORYTELLING
CREATIVE THINKING	MOTIVATING	SUMMARIZING
DANCING	NEGOTIATING	TAKING PICTURES
DEBATING	ORGANIZING	TEACHING
DECORATING	PAINTING	TEAM-BUILDING
DESIGNING	PERSUADING	TELLING JOKES
DIRECTING	PLAYING AN INSTRUMENT	TRAVELING
DRAWING	PLAYING SPORTS	TUTORING
EDITING	PUBLIC SPEAKING	TYPING
		WRITING

• What things not listed here do you enjoy doing?

• Which three skills or interests are your favorite?

• How might you use these talents and passions to make a difference?

GETTING THE WORD OUT

When people want to get hold of me quickly, the best way to reach me is:

☐ by e-mail   (my address: _____)

☐ by text message   (my number: _____)

☐ by home phone   (my number: _____)

☐ by cell phone   (my number: _____)

☐ by mail   (my address: _____

                              _____)

☐ in person

Other ways I get information include:

☐ church newsletter

☐ bulletin board

☐ e-mail news announcements

☐ fliers

☐ personal invitation

☐ announcements during worship service or youth group

☐ the church or youth group website

☐ other

CELEBRATION AND RECOGNITION

The way I most like to be recognized for hard work is:

___ a party in my honor

___ getting a note or e-card

___ seeing my name in print (in a newspaper or church newsletter or on the Web)

___ seeing my picture in print

___ getting an award or certificate (something I can put on my wall)

___ a simple thank you

___ balloons or candy

___ being verbally recognized in front of a group of peers

___ being verbally recognized in front of a group of adults

___ a hug

___ something sentimental, such as a scrapbook of photos, a special souvenir, or a framed photo

___ other ways:

Under each category, list three things that you love.

Things that are free:

1.

2.

3.

Things that cost $5 or less:

1.

2.

3.

Things that cost $1 or less:

1.

2.

3.

Candy, snacks, or treats:

1.

2.

3.

MY MOTIVATION

Which of the following factors motivate you to get involved in service and make a difference in the world? (Check all that apply.)

___ My friends are involved.

___ The service project involves an issue I care about.

___ I may have the opportunity to meet new people and make new friends.

___ I'm bored and don't have anything better to do.

___ Helping others makes me feel good.

___ I'm honored that someone asked me to participate.

___ I need service experience to put on a college, scholarship, or honor-society application.

___ I have gifts and talents that I can contribute to the project.

___ I just like to be involved.

___ Serving others is the right thing to do.

___ I want to be recognized by my friends and peers.

___ I want to experience new things and go new places.

___ Friends and family members have encouraged me to be involved.

___ I want adults to recognize me and be proud of me.

___ I feel that God is calling me to be involved in service.

___ I just want to make a difference; I can help.

READY-TO-GO SERVICE PROJECTS

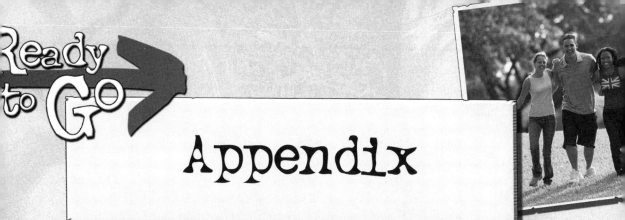

Appendix

SAMPLE PROJECT TIMELINES

TIMELINE FOR A "CRAWL" PROJECT

Example: serving dinner at a rescue mission or homeless shelter

5–6 Weeks Out

→ Determine the time and date.

→ Contact the mission or shelter, and find out whether your time and date will work.

→ Confirm logistics, such as age requirements, dress, expectations, and supplies.

→ Visit the site to make sure that it is safe and that meaningful projects are available.

3–4 Weeks Out

→ Recruit adult chaperones.

→ Get the word out: Put an announcement in the youth group newsletter, the church bulletin, and the church and youth group websites.

→ Educate the group about the causes and problems related to homelessness. Tell the youth the details about the project and what you'll be doing.

1–2 Weeks Out

→ Ask volunteers to sign up for the project.

→ Coordinate group transportation.

→ Remind the volunteers about the dress code, inclement weather, and other relevant project details.

→ Gather any needed supplies.

Days to Go

→ Call the organization to make sure that they are expecting you and to see whether there are any last-minute changes.

Day Of

→ Prepare and serve dinner to the homeless men and women.

→ Afterward, discuss your experience.

Days and Weeks Later

→ Tell others about what you have done and what you have learned from the project.

→ Determine other ways you could address the issue of homelessness.

TIMELINE FOR A "WALK" PROJECT

Example: hosting a field day for the Boys & Girls Club

5–6 Weeks Out

→ Convene a leadership team to plan the event.

→ Work with the Boys & Girls Club to set the date, time, and place.

→ Ask the Boys & Girls Club what kinds of activities would be good for a field day.

→ Make arrangements with the venue where the event will be held, if you need to do so.

→ Visit the site and determine what opportunities it provides and what obstacles it poses.

3–4 Weeks Out

→ Decide on specific field-day activities, and determine volunteer staffing needs.

→ Recruit adult chaperones.

→ Get the word out: Put an announcement in the youth group newsletter, the church bulletin, and the church and youth group websites.

→ Talk with the group about Christ's compassion for children (using Scriptures such as **Luke 18:15-17**) and the mission of the Boys & Girls Clubs of America.

1–2 Weeks Out

→ Make a supply list, and gather needed supplies.

→ Invite the volunteers to sign up for the project; work with them to identify how they can best use their gifts and passions to meet your staffing needs.

→ Host a volunteer orientation so that the volunteers can learn the details of what they'll be doing, and ask any questions about their responsibilities.

→ Coordinate group transportation.

Days to Go

→ Remind the volunteers about project details, dates, and times.

→ Call the Boys & Girls Club to see whether there are any last-minute changes.

Day Of

→ Host the field day.

→ Discuss your experience.

Days and Weeks Later

→ Tell others about what you have done and what you have learned from the project.

→ Determine other ways you could help children in your community.

TIMELINE FOR A "RUN" PROJECT

Example: teaching a 6-week basic computer class at the community center

6–7 (or More) Weeks Out

→ Convene a leadership team to plan the class.

→ Work with the community center to set the dates, time, and place for the class.

→ Ask the community center what computer skills would most benefit the people whom the center serves.

→ Visit the community center, and determine what opportunities it provides and what obstacles it poses. Consider the number of computers, what software is on the computers, whether the facility has an LCD projector, and so on.

→ Work with the community center to design and implement a plan to let the community know about the class.

→ Determine your volunteer staffing needs. Roles for volunteers may include instructors, assistants, greeters, registration coordinators, and publicity coordinators.

3–5 Weeks Out

→ Recruit volunteers to fill the roles you've identified.

→ Identify the lead instructor for each lesson.

→ Work with the instructors to outline lesson plans.

→ Hold a volunteer orientation session to talk about the clientele, teaching expectations, and so forth.

→ Check all the equipment that you'll be using to be sure it is working correctly.

1–2 Weeks Out

→ Make a supply list, and gather the supplies.

→ Coordinate group transportation.

→ Call the participants to confirm their participation; let them know of any supplies they need to bring.

Days to Go

→ Remind volunteers about project details, dates, times, and locations.

Day Of

→ Teach the class.

→ Talk about your experience.

Days and Weeks Later

→ Tell others about what you have done and what you have learned from the project.

→ Determine other ways you could help children in your community.

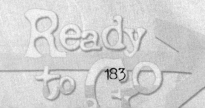

SERVICE-LEARNING SCRIPTURES

Matthew 20:27-28: "Whoever wishes to be first among you must be your slave; just as the Son of Man came not to be served but to serve, and to give his life a ransom for many."

Acts 20:35: "In all this I have given you an example that by such work we must support the weak, remembering the words of the Lord Jesus, for he himself said, 'It is more blessed to give than to receive.'"

Galatians 5:13-14: For you were called to freedom, brothers and sisters; only do not use your freedom as an opportunity for self-indulgence, but through love become slaves to one another. For the whole law is summed up in a single commandment, "You shall love your neighbor as yourself."

Ephesians 6:7-8: Render service with enthusiasm, as to the Lord and not to men and women, knowing that whatever good we do, we will receive the same again from the Lord, whether we are slaves or free.

1 Peter 4:10-11a: Like good stewards of the manifold grace of God, serve one another with whatever gift each of you has received. Whoever speaks must do so as one speaking the very words of God; whoever serves must do so with the strength that God supplies, so that God may be glorified in all things through Jesus Christ.

1 John 3:18: Let us love, not in word or speech, but in truth and action.

ADDITIONAL RESOURCES

ORGANIZATIONS TO SUPPORT YOUR WORK

→ **The Center for Asset Development,** *www.theassetedge.net,* offers play days, retreats, training, and curriculum development to help schools, churches, and other youth-serving agencies embrace the best practices in youth work.

→ **Do Something,** *www.dosomething.org,* is a nationwide network of youth making a difference in their communities.

→ **Idealist.org: Action Without Borders** has a Kids and Teens page, *www.idealist.org/kt,* offering resources and tools to start service-learning projects, as well as and links to websites that provide perspective on human rights, the environment, and the arts.

→ **Kids Care Clubs,** *www.kidscare.org,* is a volunteer network of groups made up of kids eighth-grade or younger. Kids Care Clubs provide project ideas, grant opportunities, and training for schools, churches, and community organizations.

→ **Learn and Serve America,** *www.learnandserve.org,* provides funding and training support for service-learning programs in schools, community-based organizations, and colleges

→ **Learn and Serve America's National Service-Learning Clearinghouse,** *www.servicelearning.org,* offers a compilation of curriculum, funding sources, and toolkits for service-learning practitioners.

→ **Learning in Deed,** *www.learningindeed.org,* has resources for everyone from the novice to the expert. Learning in Deed offers networking opportunities, a list of service-learning websites, and ideas for implementing service-learning projects.

→ **Learning to Give,** *www.learningtogive.org,* has a collection of faith-based and secular resources, topical project ideas, and curriculum to promote youth philanthropy and service.

→ **National Service-Learning Partnership,** *www.service-learning partnership.org,* brings together practitioners, administrators, policy makers, researchers, and community leaders to support service-learning.

→ **National Youth Leadership Council,** *www.nylc.org,* offers tip sheets, peer mentoring, and networking opportunities for people in the service-learning field.

→ **Points of Light Foundation,** *www.pointsoflight.org,* engages people in volunteer service to help solve serious social problems.

→ ***Servenet.org*** matches volunteers with local organizations in need of help.

→ **Youth Service America,** *www.ysa.org,* promotes service-learning, and challenges youth to commit themselves to a lifetime of service, learning, leadership, and achievement.

NATIONAL EVENTS

Connecting to a national event increases the scope and impact of your project. Your youth can participate with other volunteers and organizations around the country; they can travel to other cities. Being a part of something big—something that involves thousands of people gathered for one cause—energizes your group. Here are some occasions for service celebrated in the United States:

January

→ Martin Luther King, Jr. Day, *www.mlkday.org*
  Vision: to keep Martin Luther King, Jr.'s legacy of service alive across the country

April

→ Global Youth Service Day, *www.ysa.org/nysd*
  Vision: to empower young people and encourage them to volunteer

→ National Volunteer Week, *www.pointsoflight.org/programs/seasons/nvw*
  Vision: to recognize and celebrate the efforts of volunteers

May

→ Join Hands Day, *www.joinhandsday.org*
  Vision: to bring youth and adults together to improve communities

September

→ My Good Deed Day, *www.mygooddeed.org*
  Vision: to encourage people to help others in honor of those who lost their lives during the 9/11 terrorist attacks against the United States

October

→ Kids Care Week, *www.kidscare.org*
  Vision: to empower kids to reach out and help others

→ Make a Difference Day, *www.usaweekend.com/diffday*
  Vision: to inspire and reward volunteers

November

→ Family Volunteer Day, *disney.go.com/disneyhand/familyvolunteers*
  Vision: to challenge families to volunteer together to strengthen their communities

RECOGNITION PROGRAMS

→ **The Congressional Award,** *www.congressionalaward.org*
This United States Congress award program is open to all 14- 23-year-olds.
Participants earn bronze, silver, or gold Congressional Award certificates
and medals. Attaining each level involves setting and meeting goals in
four program areas: volunteer public service, personal development,
physical fitness, and expedition or exploration.

→ **Daily Point of Light Award,** *www.pointsoflight.org/awards/dpol/*
This award is designed to honor those who have made a commitment to
bringing people together to meet critical needs in their communities. The
Points of Light and Hands On Network honors one volunteer per
weekday as the "Daily Point of Light."

→ **The President's Volunteer Service Awards,**
www.presidentialserviceawards.gov
Any student who contributes at least 50 hours (ages 14 and under) or
100 hours (ages 15 to 25) to his or her community is eligible for this
award. A student's school, college, or community organization can certify
his or her service hours.

→ **The Prudential Spirit of Community Awards,**
www.prudential.com/view/page/public/12847
Sponsored by Prudential Financial, Inc., these awards honor middle school
and high school students who have exhibited exemplary, self-initiated
community service. Schools may select one honoree per every 1,000
students. The Prudential recognizes students at a local, state, and national
level.

FOR YOUR BOOKSHELF

→ *Beyond Leaf Raking: Learning to Serve, Serving to Learn,* by Peter L. Benson and Eugene C. Roehlkepartain (Abingdon Press, 1993)

→ *Blue Like Jazz: Nonreligious Thoughts on Christian Spirituality,* by Donald Miller (Thomas Nelson, 2003)

→ *Compassion: A Reflection on Christian Life,* by Henri J.M. Nouwen, Donald P. McNeill, and Douglas A. Morrison (Image, 2005)

→ *Conspiracy of Kindness: A Unique Approach to Sharing the Love of Jesus With Others,* by Steve Sjogren (Regal Books, 2008)

→ *Don't Waste Your Life,* by John Piper (Crossway Books, 2003)

→ *Great Group Games: 175 Boredom-Busting, Zero-Prep Team Builders for All Ages,* by Susan Ragsdale and Ann Saylor (Search Institute Press, 2007)

→ *Lifekeys: Discover Who You Are,* by Jane A.G. Kise, David Stark, and Sandra Krebs Hirsch (Bethany House, 2005)

→ *Ministries of Mercy: The Call of the Jericho Road,* by Timothy J. Keller (P&R Press, 1997)

→ *Ministry and Spirituality: Creative Ministry, the Wounded Healer, Reaching Out,* by Henri J.M. Nouwen (Continuum International Publishing Group, 1996)

→ *Ready-to-Go Missions: 12 Complete Plans for Life-Changing Experiences,* by Jason Schultz (Abingdon Press, 2006)

→ *Religion in Shoes: Brother Bryan in Birmingham,* by Hunter Blakely (John Knox Press, 1953)

→ *Restoring At-Risk Communities: Doing It Together and Doing It Right,* by John M. Perkins (Baker Books, 1996)

→ *The Complete Guide to Service Learning: Proven, Practical Ways to Engage Students in Civic Responsibility, Academic Curriculum, and Social Action,* by Cathryn Berger Kaye (Free Spirit Publishing, 2003)

→ *The Kid's Guide to Service Projects: Over 500 Service Ideas for Young People Who Want to Make a Difference,* by Barbara A. Lewis (Free Spirit Publishing, 1995)

→ *The Kid's Guide to Social Action: How to Solve the Social Problems You Choose—And Turn Creative Thinking Into Positive Action,* by Barbara A. Lewis (Free Spirit Publishing, 1998)

CONTACT THE AUTHORS

If you would like to know more about service-learning or have
questions about incorporating learning and reflection into your
group's next service project, e-mail your questions to authors
Susan Ragsdale (susan@theassetedge.net) and **Ann Saylor**
(ann@theassetedge.net). You can also visit the Center for Asset
Development's Website at *www.assetedge.net* and read Susan and
Ann's blog at *apps.theassetedge.net/blog/*.

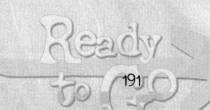

Ready to Go

Notes